Liberation
Economics

SPIRITUALITY IN SUPPLY AND DEMAND
SECOND EDITION

G U Y   W I L D W O O D

Visual meditations: Jo Lee Wood

First impression: 2024
Updated version: 2026

© Copyright Guy Wood and Y Lolfa Cyf., 2024

Cover design: Y Lolfa

ISBN: 978-1-80099-814-8

Published and printed in Wales
on paper from well-maintained forests by
Y Lolfa Cyf., Talybont, Ceredigion SY24 5HE
website www.ylolfa.com
e-mail ylolfa@ylolfa.com
tel 01970 832 304

'Man knows that the world is not made on a human scale; and he wishes that it were.'
André Malraux

'Happiness makes up in height
for what it lacks in length.'
Robert Frost

Overview

This book looks at the cultural context in which economic decisions are typically taken in the West and now increasingly globally. It considers how economic activity may be rendered increasingly proportionate, sustainable – and fairer – by involving, more openly, the spiritual dimension. I draw predominantly on my own Christian heritage but other traditions too are called upon. I take each to be a culturally-particular version of the universal. The selection is personal, and I trust to the point. Although I would always separate the teachings of Jesus from the religious institution that grew up after him, it is not my purpose here to get involved in doctrinal disputes, or to start wearing badges. I simply say that for a religious establishment to stress the inculcation of a belief structure (and too literally) over the emergence of our inborn higher potential, our ascendance, is either suspect or a missed opportunity.

My conception of the 'spiritual' is broad. Indeed, if human life is to continue into the medium-, let alone the long-term, much more than an intermittent cognitive connection with the nature of life, and especially with that entity that is the Earth, seems necessary. Yet there are many ways by which we are side-tracked or seduced away from this awareness.

Within this brief overview, employing non-technical terms as far as I am able, I weigh up the basic economic models and work structures. The old question of how best to combine human freedom with community inevitably comes up. My emphasis is not on superficial definitions of these concepts, but rather on how these interests coincide at a deeper level. Even in ancient Rome, hothouse of ambition, no citizen's success could be allowed to rival the glory of the Republic.

Money, that rather ambiguous creation, is scrutinised.

Something that represents something else can never, of course, be that thing. The perils of living within abstractions are noted, as are some business shenanigans. A section on consumerism follows. This de facto creed has still to be seriously challenged, beyond a few perfunctory utterances. *Au contraire*, you are practically an Enemy of the People if you do not troop into the malls, physically or 'virtually', and spend. Some will even attempt, with dogged persistence, to buy the things money cannot proverbially buy, including enlightenment and 'salvation', without having received them through blessing or personal change. It is the stuff of farce and tragicomedy.

A more encompassing, spiritual, outlook will naturally have something to contribute, but I hope with compassion rather than condemnation. We have had enough of people being hectored.

Politics is inseparable from economics. The proper function of government is contrasted with controlling, anti-democratic forces that seek to infiltrate it (or even prevent an authentic democratic choice being available in the first place). The negative side of the relationship between bigger business and the State – a cosy arrangement of mutual interests – is notorious. Socialist thinking would also point to the fact that the individuals with real power in both camps typically come from the same social class – that deal on the golf course. The explosion of Wi-Fi throughout society – part of the whole Microwave Frequency (MF) communications free-for-all – is offered as a contemporary example of who really calls the tune. We have one more serious, anthropogenic threat to public health. Our identity as beings is eroded by it, physically, psychologically and culturally, yet we are informed that there is nothing to see here. The corporation plays its part in the pervasive authoritarianism, which culminates in the regime as chief belief. Difference between 'Left' and 'Right' dissolves further.

Along the way, matters such as globalisation, clandestine markets, education and the media are touched upon, but the possibly more unexpected subjects of music, competitive sport, sociopathy, diet, litter and pets also make an appearance. Observations on the Welsh experience, including those to do with cultural imposition, are floated.

Basic socio-economic principles are not ignored. Guided by these, instances of bias, assumptions that are wearing out, and general ideational inertia are highlighted. This is a salutary exercise, providing protection against the wrong questions being formulated, and so many elegant, clever, but superfluous models being churned out. Too many professional economists, it seems, support, possibly unwittingly, an old world. Perhaps they are quite happy with their place in it, but intellectual heroism this is not. Welcoming a spiritual perspective to the table must result in the expansion of the slender (and pessimistic) conception of *homo economicus*.

In my conclusion I suggest a few things to help propel us out of our present state – using our latent strengths and beginning from where we are. 'We' is a word I use a lot.

Utopian thinking is avoided. It is glib to say that the answer lies in higher consciousness, as this is not entirely in our gift. From my point of view, a habit, a norm, of deeper personal reflection and a reading of the signs have to be enough – as a start. These are simply matters of self-respect; there is no dignity whatsoever in choosing illusion. And one can always be encouraged to dispose of the fag-end of a reality. Each of us is Odysseus trying to get home. This book wishes to be a part of the return to ourselves.

Contents

Introduction

Having the conversation

Welcome.

We have now created the Hypereconomy, whose consequences the Earth cannot support. Our relationship with the natural world has become one of rape and hurt, instead of symbiosis. There is a fascination with the 'can' over the 'should/should not'. Harm can only come around to us, of course. The warnings have been there for those who wish to think. Believing that one can exist in separation is a dangerous delusion. Society, too, is stressed into sickness by an economy revved up to screaming. However, capitulating at the prospect of various types of catastrophe is not necessary, for there is so much we can do, minus panic. Spiritually, this is crisis as opportunity, that one half of life.

Yet spirituality is not much in evidence in the practice of economics. If it were picked out, I imagine it being seen to be left behind, or knocked over in the rush. Is this really any surprise, though? In Abraham Maslow's hierarchy, basic needs require satisfaction before the higher faculties can be engaged, do they not? Just as a subsistence economy precedes one with a service sector. We need bread on the table. As one desire is satisfied, though, another appears. We are creatures of open-ended wants, which is both an impulsion and a frustration. One is drawn on, nevertheless.

Sadly, the spiritual facet of ourselves is not prized in contemporary life. On the contrary, its appearance is likely to provoke scorn and suspicion. In this atmosphere a splitting of the self is likely, hobbling the individual, and preventing decisions being made with the fullest input. The whole is unable to be greater than the sum of its parts. In my own Christian tradition – if this is not a caricature – the spirit has its own domain. The popular imagination has the blessed, shriven soul in Paradise, a state of being contrasting with the ordeal of this tragic world. It has found its belonging. The mire, snares, and all this 'earthly dross' are left behind. Nothing down here is worth behaving badly for. Even with laughter, which we welcome, and seek, there is a problem. Vulnerability and the gap between aspiration and achievement are everywhere. If so much humour is rooted in the sense of relief experienced when we realise that something bad is not happening to us but to someone else, then what does this say about this place? Mirth is a manager of fear, and more widely is about the release of tension. When the clowns' car comes lolloping into the circus ring, I always laugh as the driver makes to get out and the door falls off (timing crucial). Then another character is walking around in those long, red, flapping shoes with the bulbous ends. These are profound (visual) philosophical statements that go as deep as you are able to follow them.

Nutrition, too, raises concern. Unless we are fruitarians – or breatharians – other life is taken so that we may live. From how I am able to see it, the prospect is not good for a paradise on earth as we know it. Will the plagues and natural disasters disappear? What are we going to do with the British weather? It is like living with a depressed person. The fastidious might also point out the tendency for everything in the physical world to get dirty or to become surrounded by detritus. Being dumped on from the sky by a passing bird adds insult to injury. Somehow, I cannot picture washing machines or vacuum cleaners in heaven. More seriously, would one be content to continue with the sheer limitation of body and mind? Or being caught up in time? To be here and then to be gone, like summer laughter carried away on the breeze.

And if, according to Gnostic thought, the world is a malign illusion in which we are prisoners, in body shame to boot, the challenge is a little more serious. As it is if we turn out to be a genetically-engineered mishmash in a bigger, and unknown, project. Then there is the question of whether the mass incidence of human depression, clinical and sub-clinical, along with its related set of self-destructive behaviours, is bound up with the profound feeling that this place is not 'home'. (All three subjects being no-go areas at educational institutions.)

Typically regarded as a destination or, in the Christian view, a future event to take place on earth, 'heaven' should also be seen as moving within a profound congruity – by definition not a solitary experience. A little like being carried by the Adagio of Bach's 'Concerto for violin and oboe in D minor', BWV 1060 – music of pure flow and spaciousness. You worked through the karma and got home. Only the Bodhisattva puts the return off. 'Reward' is intrinsic to actions taken and experienced in the moment. It is not received at some kind of passing-out parade from a decorated figure on a podium.

An artistic medium can carry more information. The literal is not how Jesus taught.

Philosophically, we cannot come to a definitive judgement of earthly reality; all the information is not available. This lack must be endured, to be compensated for by an art of living. Spirituality knows of the deeper good in existence. It certainly distinguishes between value and price. Those signed up to religions must trust that they are not tried beyond their own limits. These remain big asks of us, though; it is easier to slip into hating life. For sure, one cannot avoid the accumulation of ailments with ageing; they are a bit like a collection of ugly figurines in the lounge.

'Living is an illness to which sleep provides relief every sixteen hours. It's a palliative. The remedy is death.' Nicolas-Sébastien Chamfort (1741–94).

*

Amongst the spiritual warrior cadres vows of poverty, and practices such as fasting, along with more direct mortifications of the flesh, are laid out as the way. The material plane is to be transcended for something greater, a realm of inner radiance and colours that are other. However, too enthusiastic a renunciation will rub up against the divine view of Creation as good. The tension between the worlds is there and must be negotiated. I should remember this when I find the coarseness of 'down here' infra dignitatem. There is also all the difference between working with whatever circumstances or emotions present – for understanding – and merely trying to expunge them. Spirituality is not simply to be found in the cerebral, either. For some, what is vital is discovered through a celebration of the physical, by way of spontaneity, risk and wilder behaviours. These are not necessarily selfish or indulgent. Dance is worth citing. The Dionysian complements the Apollonian; it is not either/or but both/and.

Where there are the big questions, spirituality is to be found. It usually takes these not head-on, but obliquely. It is beyond psychology and philosophy but will embrace some of the concepts of both. The spiritual life is going to beckon at some stage. However, I believe it a mistake to over-formalise and fix the insights, experiences and speculations that constitute it, as in a glowering doctrine. It is to be more like riding a wave. If, following philosopher Karl Popper, all knowledge is provisional, then this must apply to fields other than science. Outlooks, like fashions, rise and fall, with new versions replacing the old. When the current batch fades out there will not be any fuss. Note that human beings will demand, summon or create an interpretation of their reality; whether the reading is right or wrong is of secondary importance!

Matter and spirit may be seen together in indigenous traditions, in the phenomenon known as animism. Then there is the doctrine of pantheism – God as the universe. Scientific support of a sort comes from physicist Max Planck:

'I regard consciousness as fundamental. I regard matter as derivative from consciousness. We cannot get behind consciousness. Everything that we talk about, everything that we regard as existing, postulates consciousness.'

Also, one comes across the notion/belief that the Divine is the state of all possibility, from which we are birthed and to which we return. These are differing world views with enormous implications and consequences for everyday choices.

*

Inevitably it is difficult for the spiritual to be carried by words, as language is disjunctive and earthbound. Moreover, according to Nietzsche, 'words make the uncommon common'. Notwithstanding, and 'through a glass, darkly' (1 Corinthians 13:12), I will take it to be a force in addition to the superficies, finer and transporting. It is free-flowing, makes unexpected appearances and is often inconvenient.

The matter of spirituality is devolved to the individual. Its root is here, and how common it is within the group will be a macroeconomic variable.

If those from the materialistic paradigm do not somehow engage with the spiritual within (or whatever term is preferred), their accounts of human affairs will be incomplete. Science would do well to be alerted, by multiple-witness testimony, to phenomena for which it has, on its own terms, no current satisfactory explanation. As a discipline it is there to serve knowledge, not cosset careers, or defend, *à outrance*, one epistemological model.

Re the economy, spiritual theologian Matthew Fox observes that when there is spiritual starvation, resort is made to violence and addiction. There is pathos in that shrunken, dangling and solitary party balloon.

Spirituality can overlap, to a greater or lesser extent, religion. However, glimpses of transcendence easily ossify into codifications. It has been observed that those who succeed the foundational figure seldom have the inspiration. Too much communication, not enough communing. Things turn more towards a response to the anxiety of uncertainty, which will also take in religion substitution. Dogma appears, and formalism is the practice. Neither of these is to be pushed, however, considering the interiority of religious experience. After Jesus, Paul went off in a direction of his own. Many more versions of who Jesus was would follow. Followers, too often, are smug and closed. Their talk, with its foregone conclusion, reminds me of car salesmen. The vehicle, as it were, may be mistaken for the destination, the means for the end. And is over-identification with the first a version of idolatry? Another worry is that a belief group, whose members routinely validate each other over a pre-existent set of views, will lend itself to becoming a *folie à deux* on a grand scale.

When it comes to worship, culminating in, it has to be said, a miserable servility (strangely mirroring earthly power realities), it would be better for the accent to be on reverence and admiration instead. These make up a healthier relationship. Denigration in the form of self-abasement serves no good purpose.

And when taking on meaning, there is always the question of the reliability of the teaching's transmission, including fidelity of translation to text.

Some do not need the repetition to which congregants are subject, or want a religion that fears human freedom more than it is able to embrace it philosophically. (Adam's disobedience was going to happen, was it not?) May your way be guided by something *alive*. 'Draw nigh to God, and he will draw nigh to you' (James 4:8). I hope to show how the spiritual is the context for the economic.

The question of faith needs untangling. It cannot be founded on mere say-so, especially where the latter is more a projection onto reality than an interpretation of it. The devotion and steadfastness that comprise faith require a deeper source, together with periodic positive feedback. It is about not being boxed-in unnecessarily. There is an adaptive humility which, when flexed, leads one to walk towards events, even playfully. Faith is to be a relationship, not a competition (especially with oneself). God being nearer to us than we are to ourselves is worth much pondering.

Belief is only the beginning. Proclaiming mere beliefs will not get us very far, in particular if these are really only more possessions.

We have all run into, and too many times, those 'no man cometh unto the Father, but by me' religious codes, as ordinarily preached, which often seem to serve, pre-eminently, the psychological needs of those touting them, instead of being an open proffering to others. The gospel, the good news, is grabbed at, and rendered dragging and unbeautiful.

I don't want to enter a refuge for those who have not been able to make friends with the world. Haughty but fragile, and criticising things for what they are not, these evangelists are an instance of life-expression turned back on itself – hence their general heaviness and the terrible boredom they induce. Where there is no mutual respect, and humility, there can be no relationship of course. For their information, the superior path of evangelism is to personally possess the concomitant demeanour, manner, and aura to which people instinctively wish to get closer. Ones bearing is able to transmit a world of significance, elegantly and entire.

It can be argued that human beings do not need a religion so much as a meaning and a vista. Aspiration is still encouraged. A human construct is always less than the reality anyway. In the world, rulers and other powerful entities may attempt infiltration of the religious organisation in order to produce a tool of control and oppression based on distortion.

Sadly, the idea that we are not worthy, either by comparison or in and as ourselves, plays into this. Consider, for example, the old issue of threats of damnation from the pulpit – piling on top of 'original sin' – to cow the congregation. I prefer to view 'Hell' as separation from God. The question is whether this distance ever need be permanent.

'I count religion but a childish toy,
And hold there is no sin but ignorance.'
Christopher Marlowe, *The Jew of Malta* (*c*.1592)

The mystical heart of the message gets covered, and devotees are kept locked outside in a stasis of deference. Study of whether this has occurred, and if so to what extent, complements an intuitive approach to the authenticity of the teaching. Consult the Bible as a seeker, but with calm caution. There is Hitler's claim to the efficacy of the big lie, but what about the notion that the best propaganda always contains some truth? It could be mostly truth.

A functioning society has ethics and rules, but the secular

and spiritual can, in daily reality, seem more complementary than integrated; they may even become compartmentalised. But even the metropolitan atheist should get that Christianity is the foundation of Western freedoms and subsequently of modern material choice.

I am with Gandhi when he says: 'A religion that takes no account of practical affairs and does not help to solve them is no religion.'

*

On a daily basis we are compelled to choose between competing demands. The hero torn between (romantic) love and duty is a staple of opera – Don José in *Carmen*, Radamès in *Aida*, Octavio in *Giuditta*. Some values will be non-negotiable. It may not make for good melodrama, but picking our way through, employing deft compromise, need not be a disgrace. Indeed, this may be the best possible outcome, both from a utilitarian point of view, and in confessing uncertainty. There will always be a debate about alternatives, but those guiding stars exist. Sloppiness can lead to disaster (brilliantly exemplified on the sporting field), and a few clever but fragmented initiatives will not be enough.

If the subject of economics is said to be about the allocation of scarce resources, then we hit a couple of difficulties immediately. To designate as resources, to commodify, automatically downgrades the entities concerned, especially what we know as living beings. Respect is lost, as is connectivity, and we force ourselves into greater isolation. We fell trees for toilet paper. Then, how much of 'scarcity' is really the result of human grasping, anxiety and heedlessness? 'Spiritual Economics' is probably an oxymoron (as tortured a concept as that of an Army chaplain), but grappling with the proposal can generate some great creativity. For instance, in forms of a balancing Yin for the over-heated Yang. (Patriarchy, by definition, has little room for the sacred feminine.) Beyond a hunter-gatherer way of life, this is what faces us now.

Rationality, though good, is not enough.

The expulsion from Eden is a good story of the transition from that hunter-gathering to agriculture – and subsequent economies. The change was momentous. A plausible take on this is that our settling down as farmers led us to holding on to possessions, ending the sharing and egalitarianism of the previous society. A higher degree of conflict ensued, including erosion of the position of women. Also, a plethora of new human diseases arose from proximity to domesticated farm animals. As agriculture enabled, in time, the development of cities, infection multiplied from living in urban concentrations. Supporting oneself became tightly organised, bringing along the oppression identified by Marx. The fact is that we are simply not adapted for drudgery. Bear this massive cultural wrench in mind when examining the myriad contemporary personal and social ills.

*

The primary need, individually and collectively, is physical survival – the sine qua non.

Logical, stated so many times, yet somehow relegated in the list of manifest priorities. Economic activity, like some parasite that has taken over the host, continues to exhaust the Earth and destabilise the environment. The conceivable end is that life, this time our own, will be barely possible. Just how unpleasant the death-throes would be is typically not allowed into awareness, although the warning may receive passing acknowledgement. The twin problems of overpopulation (at least when Western lifestyles and consumption patterns become more and more prevalent) and pollution (both accumulated and current) could be paid a lot more than lip service, so that the planet's carrying capacity is not exceeded. We are lucky, though, to be presented with some token schemes, which not only serve as political fig leaves but, more dismaying, have something of the appearance of sympathetic magic.

We are looking at natural un-selection.

Moreover, when arrogance blinds us to our origins and dependence, there is an echo of the fall of Lucifer. And like Lucifer we lose our radiance. This narrative and its symbolism are central.

The demand on us is so much common sense (there *is* a time to preach). It is a responsibility we should relish exercising, especially if we wish to see ourselves as beings of mastery, or even grown-ups. Yet the fate of those who speak out on these matters is so easily to be viewed as whining and irrelevant, or, in the social milieu, as party-poopers. The more something is uttered, the less it is heard.

Thus we have yet to achieve a globally-supported ecological rescue plan – for that is what is needed. And an infusion of the ability to cherish. If Earth were a ship it would be one without lifeboats. Instead, we apparently prefer to devote energies to squabbling, distrust and a whole range of very secondary concerns. We have worn a path for ourselves, and it is difficult to get off it. And for some the game may be the chief reality. 'He who dies with the most toys wins', that idiot declaration.

To be fair though, perhaps the free-rider principle is at work here too. This is where, in hoping for a desired outcome, an individual does not alter his or her behaviour, trusting / assuming that others will. Maybe there is more of a self-centred gamble in play.

I also wonder how much of the sum of economic activity is simply the outcome of an essential restlessness, a desire to keep moving and to innovate – those human givens. I might, too, speculate about a fundamental mismatch, for whatever reason, between our nature and that of the living planet. We come 'trailing clouds of glory' but there is an uncomfortableness about being here. The need to don clothing, and the pain and danger of childbirth are but two examples staring at us – even if these are trade-offs in adaption, the first about the ability to dissipate heat, the second selecting for larger brain size. It can only be hard to live through the multiple and overlapping cycles of creation and destruction that characterise the world. One can discern sometimes a residual melancholy in many of us. Discomfort and the weakness of the body will bring forth their own economics.

However, we shall not be honoured ancestors – possibly not even ancestors at all – if we fail to step-up now. (One of the first acts in medicine is to stabilise the patient.) This is if Gaia, the Earth goddess and great Mother, has not become completely exasperated by us.

*

Since that now rather distant degree in Economics I have kept up my interest, on and off. Fortuitously, putting down a subject for a while can result in different perspectives, and inflows of ideas from many other areas. Nevertheless, in beginning this piece I do not know where it is going to lead exactly, and that is fine. A case of the path being no path?

Intellectual reviews ought to be undertaken periodically anyway. Concepts and theories that no longer fit are to be – gloriously – jettisoned. The inconvenient questions must be neither ducked nor glossed. If this philosophical standard can be met then, at the very least, one is not going to go down looking ridiculous or useless, for posterity is a harsh judge.

In this work my adherence will be towards higher-level concepts such as proportion and harmony, together with a respect for the pre-existence of the whole. In harmonising you do not have to work everything out. 'Yes', 'no' or 'maybe' come as feedback, in a process similar to the testing of a hypothesis in science.

I advocate rational caution in situations of uncertainty but remain open to the possibility of other forms of knowing. For example, just because of the relative vastness of the universe, it is a mistake to discount the possibility for immanent, non-local intimacy being one of its other characteristics. Philosopher Paul K. Feyerabend has referred to the 'narcissistic chauvinism' of science. Also, a vision would be good. However, one would need to communicate its vividity to others. Effective 'hows' to the 'whats' are a further matter.

This said though, I am mindful of the thin line between utopia and dystopia. I think it was Arthur Koestler who warned that we should be most on our guard against those who had what they thought was the best for us in mind. It is well to recall that history is littered with examples of mania, fad and other absurdities, which have tapped into a general suffering, and then taken everyone on a crazy adventure.

It would be dandy – just grand – to uncover an approach, one of those 'hows', which dropped sweetly into the circumstances. Sadly, I fear that the character of this existence is replete with lacunae, into which gaps all sorts of things fall – as readily as in our actions we fall into unworthiness. In the Jain view, life from our perspective is unavoidably disappointing, in the Buddhist inescapably impermanent. Where 'The day soon clouds o'er'. Where 'Nothing gold can stay' (Robert Frost). It is reminiscent of one of those fruit cakes with too few cherries in it. This primes humans for bad behaviour, and bloodshed will never be far away. The jumble and tumult of our minds paired with such a frail body requires its own health warning. Exiting this bubble may have to be through suicide, in a parallel to constructive dismissal.

And from Job: 'Man that is born of woman is of few days, and full of trouble. He cometh forth like a flower and is cut down: he fleeth also as a shadow, and continueth not.'

There is money to be made in insurance.

The position is compounded by the anxiety states, phobias,

23

addictions, depression and such that can be traced to birth trauma. The other book-end, as it were, is being tortured on one's deathbed by regret.

All the songs, too, that recognise the many sides of the struggle and name them. Apart from the obvious 'I Am A Man Of Constant Sorrow', and our folk tradition of irony-tragedy, I am picking out 'Autumn Leaves', 'Buongiorno Tristezza' and 'Me and Bobby McGee', for telling it – while still hanging in there.

On the upside, not knowing keeps us engaged and makes human friendship possible. Obviously, too, the economy is built on a prior state that actually produced us and has sustained us. The organisation and development of this benevolence is the matter of economics.

Nevertheless, one of the real tragedies of the place is that for the female of our species there is a one-sided energy investment in the gestation of offspring combined with another differential, that of the male, generally, possessing a more domineering physical strength. A lament may be as pointless as complaining about the weather, but the consequence of this one-two has been untold human woe, including some of the economic variety.

Our land, further, is that of Uroboros, the serpent consuming its own tail, where the term 'the human condition' should be changed to 'the human predicament'. Where love has to make itself vulnerable. We walk around carrying unshed tears, craving magic and miracle. Magicians draw me in, even if I know it's only a show. Is there, when using that other sight, really a darkness fringing everything in this world? Once beheld it never goes away completely. I am not coming the great psychic but there is a ubiquitous baleful energy, visible to the 'third eye', that leans in on you when you declare for the good. Interestingly, it lets you know that it knows.

I think of the temptation of Jesus in the wilderness. From Matthew: 'Again, the devil taketh him up into an exceeding high mountain, and sheweth him all the kingdoms of the world, and the glory of them; And saith unto him, All these things will I give thee, if thou wilt fall down and worship me.'

A question naturally follows, and it has been put. Why would this offer have been made if these things were not actually in our opposer's gift already? Incidentally, it is definitely an unfair contract! (The ultimate in buyer's remorse too.) This holds even if the encounter were interpreted to be a tussle with the narrow ego or the shadow side of self. The satanic impulse is more to despoil than destroy.

Yet, in order for our freedom to have meaning, does there have to be a measure of 'evil' present so that there is a choice? 'Old Nick' may not be totally on the outside after all. In philosophy Hegel has contradiction originating advance. Indeed, what would we be without the bittersweet?

In circumstances of complexity and apparent conflict one recommends optimisation, broadly based, as the goal, with the ideal retained as a value. This positive is within the wit of humanity. Sirens' songs of perfection must be recognised as such.

Seeking to implement an ideal out of true context would break us. Tired and hackneyed rallying-cries notwithstanding, we have to bring others with us. Used and let down before, no doubt, but no-one else is going to be building a better world.

So cynicism, that condition of being already defeated, and an almost inevitable inertia will both need to be overcome. Interestingly, a posited asymmetry in human behaviour shown in fearing more to lose than in wishing to gain may be explicable by the low level we are already at. The drive to survive already weights the avoidance of negatives over the gaining of positives.

*

I do not wish to take any more of the reader's time than I need to. Nor do I see why this type of book should be much longer than, say, *The Communist Manifesto*! Could the material work as non-comedic stand-up? The genre might be a hard sell. It would be better in a way if the message could be distilled to the potency of a story, symbol, or even a colour. Music is another enviable medium, although susceptible to misuse, emotionality not necessarily indicating truth. But I love the title of Rodgers and Hart's 'With A Song In My Heart'; with such a predisposition one is likely to come to dwell in more reality. Handel's 'Eternal Source of Light Divine' is a musical description of what it is to finally know.

However, all I can offer is my prose; I trust that the gravity of the subject will go some way towards making up for its shortcomings. Labouring the musical metaphor, please forgive the notes that turn out to be either a bit flat or somewhat sharp. To invite new connections, my approach is going to be free-wheeling from time to time. Happily, there are many words from friends of humanity included along the way.

Statements of the openly evident, or indications of the elephant in the room, are likely to have been included on account of their subject matter being historically suppressed. Finally, what is important is not this piece in itself, but what may flow from an engagement with it. Personally I prefer to have a curiosity response generated within me over being stuffed with the 'answers'. It is for me to decide – my right and responsibility both. If the book could prove of some help in the evolution of a world-view, or in the stirrings of a new consciousness, that would be wonderful. Its style will be conversational; indeed, it is a monologue that wishes to be a dialogue. It aspires to be nothing more than a humble bridge for the mind.

As economic agents too we are exhorted to move out of lack of knowledge or denial, through psychological discomfort if necessary, although that might be the rub. Dying to provisional identity is symbolised by the Cross. Death is the price of evolution. Acceptance immediately confers a power; the problem is now encircled psychically, and the task laid out before one.

Also to gather up the scattered pieces of the psyche. A reunion. When you are all 'here' there is no longer dread. And if there is a tendency in the universe for increasing complexity – let us not call it a 'law' as we have no justification to claim it applies throughout time and space (Hume's problem of induction in philosophy) – it is fitting for the personal to evolve towards the apex of human potential. We have, too, the ability to build within ourselves the profound ease, and protection, of 'spontaneous right action'. I agree with Aristotle that it is only virtue that produces inner freedom.

'I will lift up mine eyes unto the hills: from whence cometh my help' (Psalm 121:1).

We emerge lighter, and able to bear witness – that undervalued power. The dinner party invitations may dry up for a while (what has happened to Guy?), but we can reclaim some of our splendour. Born-again even, and no-one has a monopoly on that.

Earning

Drudgery or personal authenticity?

Our lives are based on interaction with the environment and others, and work, as we understand it, is a routine part of this involvement. Property is an outcome of work, and can be viewed, up to a point, as a layer of the individual. Property rights are typically enforced by a legal code. I would add that privacy is a natural human demand.

Trading certainly enriches life, and I see the former as an economic analogue of group strength through difference. After deliberation I am for retaining the basic functioning of the open market and the price mechanism. This organisational solution is undeniably responsive to people's demands, and does, for better and for worse, facilitate individual freedom. Wastage has more to do with consumerism than the market per se. It is difficult to contradict the view that a customer-oriented economy fits more comfortably with democracy. This is why the old Communist order in China will face a rising demand for liberal reform as capitalism and consuming burgeon.

Central planning has no feedback mechanism to compare with market price; shortage or surplus across the economy is the likely result. An informal market will then take over anyway.

The free economy must, however, always be in transition as markets rise and fall, with varying levels of unemployment, matched, in the landscape, by wasteland and dereliction, as in the US 'Rustbelt'. Crags of stained concrete, graffiti murals, abnormal silhouettes, the burned-out car, a fly-tipped fridge surreal in its new environment, and random bushes of buddleia (as purple as this prose) comprise part of a new vocabulary. But the birds are starting to sing again.

The condition is that the market is to be a system of distribution and employment, and accepted as such – not an opportunity for speculation, or a vehicle for amassing irregular fortunes and getting to exercise anti-community power. In endorsing use – not abuse – taxation policy must uphold the first and not the second.

The market, then, is necessary, but not sufficient. At the organisational level government has an enabling function that provides not only legal framework, infrastructure and environmental protection but also background R&D and support for the skills base of the workforce. It can step in with investments yielding a high social return. And, vitally, it is resorted to when the market fails.

A comprehensively planned economy might be justified temporarily, as in an emergency. Nevertheless, the people must be wary of 'temporary' measures being, in reality, permanent. Yet if one policy cannot be fulfilled it may, due to system connectivity, be sub-optimal to seek to complete all the others, in which case a new configuration will be required. In human terms State diktat could be more bearable if there were space for inventive self-employment and localised artisan enterprise.

However, any method of organisation is by definition a machine, and like all machines only useful up to its limitations. There is a threshold, the crossing of which will lead to human lives, both in the workplace and beyond, being regimented by a martinet tempo. This is alien to human being, and therefore cruel. Think of Chaplin's *Modern Times* and Lang's *Metropolis*. Such wrong-headedness is underlined by Sir James Jeans: 'The Universe begins to look more like a great thought than a great machine.'

In an organised whole with a large element of central direction, there is the question of whether initiative gets squashed along with autonomy, resulting in lower innovation. Wanting to eat their cake and have it, States running the economy in this way may come to lean on commercial espionage and product piracy.

Regarding the perception of freedom, a warning is sounded when thieves, of various sorts, are romanticised or given an amused treatment in popular culture.

*

Job design is enormously pertinent in an advanced economy. In Marxian analysis, capitalism introduces technology to improve efficiency and, naturally, to maximise profit.

The consequence can be demeaning and dreary tasks for people. The worker is alienated from the product. Thus, low job satisfaction is added to the exploitation.

Of high importance, then, is knowledge of how a particular function within an enterprise will affect a worker's humanity. Our journey is our goal, too. Even better, start with the humanness and design around that, junking the managerialist crazes. This goes with the grain and is a philosophy very likely to be rewarded. Liberation Economics indeed. Companies following this approach are likely to look and behave very differently, possibly in ways that cannot even be envisaged now. Then it is important to understand that one is remunerated for work done or being available for the task. Neither you nor your time is owned.

Related here is the concept of a Universal Basic Income (UBI). In spite of its susceptibility to being a Trojan horse (crushing paternalism and worse), it has a great chance of success. I do not want to sever the connection between contribution and ones sustenance, but even when everyone is granted expenses for a reasonable standard of living most will still choose to work for reasons of social identity and responsibility, accomplishment and camaraderie, as well as for the extra dosh. (Some of the reasons why it is not much of a life being a bludger.) UBI sends out a message of respect for each and all – you are respected until you do something that loses that respect. One consequence is likely to be a greater say in the workplace, which should mean that jobs are performed with greater efficiency. An upward pressure on working conditions is to be expected too, from workers who can always just leave. State bureaucracy should shrivel.

In the round UBI makes working attractive and effectively powers up people to construct their own society. UBI is both current and investment expenditure. It pump primes the economy – with money that is not debt money.

The system moves us in the direction of a functioning anarchism. I see much more human flourishing. However, in returning to the current modus operandi, all hope is not lost. As in an Environmental Impact Assessment in planning, or with the energy efficiency rating of appliances, human occupations could be ranked according to basic satisfactions, including workplace consultation, degree of independence, creative scope and social worth. This information would facilitate better decisions in the market. Consequently, low grade jobs, which have real costs both to individuals and society, might, finally, be better rewarded. Jobs that add nothing to, or even subtract from, social value would be unmasked too. Take the role of 'flak-catcher', there to absorb customer complaints. The company may or may not have the intention to remedy the deeper problem – it may be cheaper not to do so. If this is the case then the position, whatever its title, is a pretence, a mere lightning-rod. I would rather pick stones from the farmer's field – in the rain. Also dragged out into the light will be the assignment of pointless tasks as a means to establish and signal domination within an organisation. See David Graeber's book, *Bullshit Jobs* (2018), for a perusal of jobs that really do not have to exist.

At this point I make a plea for not such an identification of a person with their work, but mindful that we have a history of surnames indicating just this. Hierarchy would be softened. Someone is always more than a job title – as if this needs to be said. Care needs to be taken around language and its use. Philosopher Ludwig Wittgenstein stated: 'The limits of my language mean the limits of my world.' And more pointedly: 'Philosophy is a battle against the bewitchment of our intelligence by means of language.'

As far as those unattractive occupations are concerned, a type of community service, carrying the very opposite of stigma, might be a supplementary measure. In this, members of society share the work of lesser appeal (where feasible) in temporary stints – I gather not a new idea. One advantage is that it would be of therapeutic benefit to those unfortunates who believe they are better than others. Service, of course, has nothing to do with servility.

The principle is to share the burden uncomplainingly. So much thinking could be released to serve this end. And why not get to a point where work is seen as a form of praise?

Still, as it involves change – and challenge – one must expect an attack from prerogative. Not least from its newspapers and other outlets pushing its own prejudices, which are deftly disguised. The ponderous arsenal of fear, derision, mockery, partisan 'expertise' and the like is likely to be deployed automatically, and with much bluster. Those who sense, even dimly, their own inflated advantage tend to display a sharp lack of tolerance of any reminder of it. One is seldom popular holding up a mirror to another.

The work ethic has already been steered so that we make more for the money monsters. Our civilisation disapproves of not-doing, even when the work has been completed. As a consequence the individual is at risk of becoming ragged and uncentred. Infinite demands may lead us to summarise that we are not good enough. The well is poisoned.

Moreover, very few people in an organisation need to be in on the full extent of its real goals for the enterprise to be carried out successfully and continuously.

The established media, being the primary source of information, is potentially a big block, as already pointed out. When it ceases, or no longer aspires, to be an honest scrutineer of public affairs, and is instead more of a slick public relations operation for vested interests, then individuals' welfare and the whole of democracy are undermined. Indeed, those powerful interests, which like to cover all bases, very probably own the media too.

I hear pundits going round and round on the supposed cracked psychology of those 'conspiracy theorists', while no journalistic digging ever takes place into the allegations and the pesky facts. This is the sound of slamming doors. Probity and common sense dropped, scientific method cast off, and no uncomfortable questions for Power. A gang is a conspiracy fact.

Conspiracy is familiar to Economics, though. Provisions exist to deal with price collusion among producers and with monopoly in the market. One exception is OPEC, the Organisation of Petroleum-Exporting Countries, which is too big to take on directly. Theirs is a restrictive practice out in the open, but dependent importers simply have to lump the double standards. Business groups naturally will lobby for their interests, trying it on maybe, and there is a history of producers concealing the negative impacts of their products. Counterfeit goods constitute a big industry also. This is an arena not exempt from either the lower human drives or from Machiavellian cleverness. Why would one think it would be? There are, too, individuals who have a sick lack of boundaries, a glee for gain, and who press on in a devotion to a self-image.

*

In the industrial economy of ours, filling vacancies for the worst (or more menial) jobs has long depended on immigrant labour. On the demand side cheap labour was put above everything else; industry interest won out. Supply side, migratory movements, whether for opportunity, promise of some better life, or even survival, have always gone on. They are part of human history. There is one humanity seeking to live.

In spite of this service and the cultural enrichment migrant peoples also offer, their fate can too often be the ghetto and a curious invisibility (except when they are to be scapegoated). The fact that our similarities far outweigh our differences is forgotten. That which is not understood will be feared, to the detriment of all.

In 'othering', what concerns me in particular is the self-fulfilling prophecy where, through a lack of fairness and opportunity, newcomers are driven into the shadow side of the economy.

For the existing community, too, there are going to be frictions, especially if the economics of the bottom line is put before all else. As well as affecting employment opportunities and hence wage rates, a substantial and sudden influx of others will give rise to pressures on housing, services and transport, inter alia. The economically weaker will suffer – there is no doubt about this (it is a matter of number). If they do speak out about the position in which they find themselves they are likely to be subject to a 'virtue-signalling' barrage from the insulated affluent, informing them that they are knuckle-dragging bigots. (This is another game being played, to be added to Eric Berne's *Games People Play: The Psychology of Human Relationships*.) Any shortcomings in articulateness, or not using sanctioned terms, will be used to delegitimise. Necessary discussion is thereby killed off, and people are not heard. (Something similar is achieved when protests against actions taken by the State of Israel, especially concerning the Palestinians, are labelled as 'anti-Semitism'!) In addition, questions of identity and possibilities of cultural incompatibility must be considered, rather than avoided altogether. For example, religious antagonisms and any patriarchy/misogyny from incoming cultures leading to, in some settings, violence against women. What tend to be the limits on integration? People, any people, want an idea of the co-ordinates of their society – the other side of the human rights issue. Without some set of expectations here, there will be ongoing apprehension, which is easily whipped up into division. Society takes a long time to knit together. Economically speaking, the lower the trust in the community the higher will be the costs, in both time and money, of transactions. An element of primitive territoriality may be present, too. This impulse is to be managed, not wished away. The UKIP/Reform vote needs to be understood. Those populist movements arise when the people are sold an over-simplified solution, but they will also spring up when the voters have had enough of the political class following another agenda.

Listen before you condemn. If there are faults to be found they may be more to do with ignorance and fear than stark moral deficiency. Economic patterning is never far away. What appears as a racist inclination can in reality be more a contempt around social status, too. The two get conflated. Take time to discover the crux of the problem, part of which is likely to reside in you.

A poorly conceived policy on immigration, plus a lack of national conversation on the subject, will fuel antagonism and stereotyping, undercutting social cohesion. Everyone has lost. Clarity on what can be reasonably expected of incomers will support acceptance and integration; diversity then becomes a vibrancy and a strength. As an immigrant myself I know this. I cannot just trade on my Welsh ancestry.

The extent to which numbers of new arrivals translate into labour available for the economy will depend, partly, on language skills, work style and ethic, life path values, position of women in education, and so forth. An economist will look at the net benefit or loss to the economy from each newcomer. These calculations must include dependants of course. The counterpart to native discrimination is newcomers making high or excessive demands and even turning on the host country. 'The best definition of man is the ungrateful biped', Dostoevsky. Either way, there is a disrespectful relationship. Multiculturalism, that tactical retreat from Marxist universalism, can work, not least because of the golden rule ('Do unto others as you would have them do unto you'), but it is going to be fragile in practice.

Sadly there are many 'isms' that prejudge and shut out, but where racist tendencies are concerned a limiting social factor carries over from our developmental history. If survival and life prospects are embedded in a group/tribe, then outsiders will not, cannot, be accepted automatically – there is much, even everything, at stake for the vulnerable and high-maintenance entities that we are, where it can all be over in the blink of an eye. Any difference will act as a trigger, with the physical category pretty much first up. Cognition notes salient factors first, moving on to progressively finer detail in further stages. The general behavioural trait is caution from unfamiliarity. Add narcissism to the mix and one sees how far there is to even get to the starting line – for, a priori, any subdivision of people. In reproduction, though, adaptive risk is spread through genetic variation, all other things being equal. Like Carroll's Red Queen, we run to stay in the same place.

Another way out of this primal predisposition is first of all to recognise it as such, as a human given, a default setting. And if genetic variation within a race can be greater than that between it and another, what then is 'race'? Racism amounts to despising and dismissing evolutionary adaptation, and not seeing the latter's waning importance in a modern industrial environment. It is a confusion about the paths life takes. Therefore one side is not to remain in self-righteous anger, with the other demonised; the problem is more profound than that. The great crimes are perpetrated when another person's humanity is erased, and when there is overidentification with that which presents to the world. Equally, adopting the equivalent of original sin – damning one group generation after generation for the 'sins of the fathers' – is to be resisted. It is collective punishment out of time.

I do not like the term 'white privilege'. One, as it is a prejudgement (therefore being racist in its own right), and two, because it ignores other factors that marginalise, notably class membership but also education. (Physical attractiveness, on the other hand, gets waved through.) 'Majority privilege' has more explanatory power. Looking at ethnicity whilst overlooking individual character is not going to do it in the longer term.

Advantage accrues to the members of a club, so wider community bounds are to be extended to match those of geography and citizenship. We are not to compartmentalise fellow-feeling, nor is love for one to depend on hate for the other. The task is to break the duality and go higher. Peoples spending time together, in whatever setting, is prescribed to dispel any bogeyman myths about the newcomer that have grown up in separation. Sharing food is so powerful. Progress can be aided by a consciousness that begins to view all life as kin and part of the Experience. So applaud what is positive when you see it, critique what is negative – analogous to taking nutrition from foodstuffs, which does not tend to outrage us. But expect a very human reaction from people who feel that their world is being broken into or that their way of living is in jeopardy. These are not '-ists' and '-phobes' – jibes found in the lingua franca of more or less violent revolution. Sanctuary is one thing, residence quite another.

Clearly, greater global equality in standards of living will reduce the incentive to move between regions. The world economy is another climate, with highs and lows of pressure. And its forces are stronger than ad hoc barriers. A distinction is to be made between asylum seekers and economic migrants, but this is not to infer that none of the latter is in (another kind of) personal emergency. We should not be surprised that policy through military intervention and proxy war creates upheaval over wide areas. Yet the moral code does not get nullified. Let there be due process. Concerning illegal immigration, I have yet to see a percentage breakdown of the figures between, on the one hand, those escaping political or sectarian violence, and on the other, the chancers and adventurers. People-trafficking is also a business. Sadly, consideration of the entirety of the data, including that on national capacity and the consequences down the line for civil health, does not appear to be a feature of current public discourse. Any proposals that do emerge would, naturally, be put to a vote.

'Plato is dear to me, but dearer still is truth', Aristotle.

And at which point, as it were, does one not enter a burning building to rescue others? Not the best figure of speech, but it does present a legitimate and uncomfortable question.

Over all this there is Jesus' attitude to the outsider – one of inclusivity. It contains a teaching far deeper than an exhortation to be 'nice'. A solution is found in a sharing, of the empowering kind, at the global level, before the desperation gains momentum. Unless you are a devotee of Social Darwinism, we all know this to be the case. As *The Big Issue* would have it, 'A HAND UP, NOT A HAND OUT'.

*

Moving on to the remuneration of labour. Unfortunately, at the moment there is such a variation across the economy. This is an outcome that tends to become more pronounced over time. Money goes to money. Moreover, financial inequality is reinforced by a globalised competition in wages. The social corrosiveness of inequality has been examined well in Wilkinson and Pickett's *The Spirit Level*. Relative poverty, in addition to the absolute variety, has some startling aspects, and there are costs for everyone. Links, for example, between stress and obesity, and between violence and the search for respect need to be incorporated into official thinking. How many of these findings are going to give rise to specific policies? What is vandalism saying? We know that human beings hate exclusion and any implication they are somehow inferior. Destructive energies, directed outwardly or inwardly, *will* be called forth.

With respect to monetary rewards, there do appear to be double standards, depending on where one is in the pecking order (a depressing phrase in the human context). At the top we are told that we have to hire the best people, yet lower down wage demands must be 'realistic'. It is a scam, and Shelley's 'Song to the Men of England' exposes the version of his time.

'Men of England, wherefore plough

For the lords who lay ye low?
Wherefore weave with toil and care
The rich robes your tyrants wear?'

An old guideline, that of the top salary being no more than 'x' times the lowest, might appeal. Any figure would appear to be plucked out of the air, though, and be vulnerable to creative accountancy and the dishing out of perks. I think we need to go much further.

Hard work – chosen – would, naturally, be rewarded to scale. However, I do not see why the faculties and talents one was born with should, in a group setting, accrue excessive returns. Again, aside from an acknowledgement of factors such as income foregone in obtaining education and training, plus the direct costs incurred, along with a recognition of enterprise, I do not understand why, for example, a surgeon should be paid much more than a street-cleaner. Both are necessary for the whole, both serve each other. So, if needs be, an income tax will be progressive, and inheritance and capital gains taxes can go some way in removing entrenched inequality, that warping of national life. This is not such a contortion if other priorities are weighed. It refers to pre-industrial notions of belonging, and the individual is not crushed. Productivity is already tremendous through mechanisation, and allocation of products by price is a better fit with some measure of income equality.

I accept that this is going to require a different relationship with the material world; one agreed, not imposed. Something not so blinkered, and definitely less terrified.

'And therein we find, neglected by us, the simplest, the most accessible key to our liberation: a personal nonparticipation in lies!' Aleksandr Solzhenitsyn, *Live Not By Lies.*

Do not seek profit from a gift. When the artist misuses the talent the Muses leave. In 1 Corinthians 10:31 we are exhorted to 'do all to the glory of God'. This is to understand.

At the macroeconomic level, less income inequality is better for sustaining a healthy GDP because money then re-enters the economy more readily as repeat expenditure. Healthier for democracy too as there will be less of an unequal surplus for buying influence, through bungs, well-connected foundations or faux philanthropy.

This egalitarianism may progress to one with stricter flows from abilities to needs. There will be those who pursue greater resources to manage simply being here. For them you cannot make a silk purse out of a sow's ear – this plane's very energy density is plain alien. The motives that emancipate us can of course engender prosperity. The pie will be big enough.

Depending on the level of incomes, more shared ownership could be seen, in order to spread the cost of investment. For instance, of some household machines, which stand unutilised for much of the time – though at the cost of convenience. The car is the obvious one. One envisages larger properties being split up into flats. Such arrangements place fewer demands on the planet.

A feature of raw nature may well be stratification, but a choice falls to us to avoid both stifling subordination and the worst of jungles. We do not accept our lot in the way animals do. A joint agreement is there to be made to protect everyone from the consequences of disorder, sans regimentation. It is a social contract. Diversity is protected, license restricted.

The subject of litter shows the tension between the individual and the group. I wonder also at the poverty of the relationship with the mother figure of Earth that its presence indicates. How did this come about? Did we drift away in our civilisations? Certainly the Divine Feminine has been historically relegated. Whatever the cause, I advocate the spontaneous picking-up of litter as a spiritual practice. And this activity, in the form of a job, I hold as nothing less than sacred service. I also suggest lying down on the Earth (facing it) periodically – forget what you look like. See what emotions or insights come. There is nothing to solve. You may receive a gift, such as heart strength or recovered knowledge.

To resume, I do not propose a rigid labour army and uniformity, but a system where people receive enough materially as the basis for thriving and growth. Eudaemonia. Natural variation would be reflected in flexibility, organically reached. Family size is a factor. It could be argued that the 'eco' number of children is one, with none ideally considered. Yet this outlook is not to shade into self-negation and animosity towards humanity itself – such will put one in the company of demons.

It is axiomatic that everyone has something to offer, and recognition that each has a valued part promotes community. Practical kindness is an investment in social capital, and relieving suffering always a fall-back meaning of life.

We are nourished by significance and belonging, where rights go with responsibilities. This socio-economic arrangement is the successor to natural, traditional groupings – tested and adaptive, they did not require rescue by 'civilisation'. Status can come from developing one's gifts to the highest degree, with an individual twist. Ideally these are spotted early.

Writer Saul Bellow has remarked: 'A man is only as good as what he loves.'

*

As you may expect, I do not envisage anything like, for example, zero-hours contracts, which leave individuals unable to plan. Nor employers' avoidance of sickness and holiday pay. There is no human solidarity here, just the features of a new serfdom, in which you come to need the unexpected to be your friend.

Instead, a living wage is the starting point. If this were implemented in this country, tomorrow, the subsidy of wages by Housing Benefit and other state entitlements would be reduced significantly. Business is on a lot of welfare already, while the collective bargaining powers of trade unions have suffered decades of political erosion. The questions are about how the condition of employee relations affects the performance of the economy, and how much we, as a body of people, want to forestall self-inflicted wounds.

I look forward to the ending of authoritarian hierarchy in the workplace too. Echoing educator Paulo Freire, I do not want one set of oppressors to replace another. The whole model requires ditching. Incidentally, this was the view of Spartacus in that eponymous revolt. It is a vision with pedigree, and goes with prayer for your enemies.

How much more liberated would be a constellation of working relationships where each individual honours commitments in a 'circle of being'. A spirit of a bona fide co-operative, transcending petty rewards and Draconian punishments. Personally, I never wish to hear the word 'boss' uttered again, not even in jest. Let it become a memory of the bad old days, like the stocks and several Seventies' sitcoms I can think of.

Out too must go the acceptability of the concept of profit. A big one, I agree. Fair return needs to be separated from profiting and profiteering. The latter pair can be judged to be forms of theft; they are void of substance. Henry Ford, in his business philosophy, got the idea of 'enough'. Fair trade is now widely supported, and the notion of the reasonable is at the heart of English civil law. Maximising behaviours can still take place but push profit out.

Trading surpluses can arise with the price mechanism operating freely in the distribution of goods and services. The consequence of higher prices is encouragement of supply, but in the shorter-term monetary surplus can be treated in a number of ways, other than it being wholly siphoned off. Utilised for selective subsidy, research and development or to absorb higher costs in a volatile market – these are all options.

Monies re-invested, or going to (certain) charitable projects, could be offset against taxation. A staff bonus is also an investment. Protocols will evolve in the wake of expectations. The crucial point is that livelihood is to be sought, not narrow, short-term, financial profit. The market will provide the signals.

It is worth remembering, too, that a product is not marked out by price alone. Input types, company ethos, innovation, style and service are all distinguishing features. However, some businesses will need to be mindful of where cultural inspiration ends and where cultural appropriation begins. A positive is that customers can push businesses towards greater moral stature.

*

A couple of other matters. First, the subject of 'externalities' cannot be skipped. These are costs, such as those of pollution, not incorporated in the price paid by the customer. A 'Pigouvian tax' – after the British economist Arthur Pigou – attempts to rectify this, and thus brings social and environmental dimensions into trading. Air travel is a good illustration of how responsibility for the full consequences of an economic activity is dodged, no doubt through a combination of party lobbying and consumer (voter) preference. Not only are there disproportionate levels of greenhouse gas emissions, but the fuel is derived from a non-renewable resource. Every party to a contract bears responsibility of course. Look up the pressure group, Plane Stupid.

I like to think that, with the majority of air travellers, it is more a case of social conditioning than greed. However, a lifestyle of flying, as opposed to occasional use, takes things to another level. Having nature's ability to cope with us in mind, psychology/psychiatry might diagnose this behaviour as childish inclination or even a death instinct (slow planetary type). To use the parlance, the primitive id is not being balanced by the calm overview of the superego. The Pleasure Principle is at the controls, not the Reality Principle. There is John Milton's phrase, 'Blind Mouths!' (from *Lycidas*). The image for me is one of a seagull gulping down a sandwich on a seaside town promenade. All those 'things to do before you die'. Which is nothing other than snouts in the trough.

Second, we need a reining-in of shareholder supremacy, with its unending pressure for returns. The bottom line fosters nothing less than a plundering and spoiling of the world.

This just validates insatiability. Legal changes will be necessary both to lead and to reflect enlightenment in commercial culture.

Ideally we would learn from the Jain practice of *ahimsa*, the rule of harmlessness. This way is not only beneficial in and of itself, but considering, for example, food provision, there is an economic pay-off too. Let's be honest – a vegetarian/vegan diet is a much more efficient method, generally, of sustaining ourselves than any other. And it does not require the grossest suffering of vast numbers of fellow sentient beings. Any involvement with meat, unless there is no choice in given circumstances, dims a person's spiritual light. However, I grant that this agriculture is not suitable for all land or its produce recommended for every human constitution.

*

These are exciting possibilities, to be given a fair hearing at least. As already mentioned though, one must expect to face, from the outset, the fiercest opposition from the old thinking. Primitive existence is about fear and attack. It is as if a pattern of thought has become a form of life in itself, and an exaggerated one at that.

*

Two final ideas. Firstly, ownership and legal title need to be distinguished. What we think of as the former is typically an instance of the latter. The claim of owning the external has no real ground to it anyway. It leads to clinging, which sets up humans royally for unhappiness. We always do well – if it is the case – to admit how hollow the things around which we organise our lives actually are. This is a kindness to the self.

Secondly, there is a question about our actual identity as beings. If all the other organisms – for example the symbiotic gut flora – that go to make us up are recognised, then that identity becomes a little blurred. If the mitochondria, those energy-generators in the cells, are bacterial in origin, then the lines get even more indistinct. At the macro-level too, we are part of a great sway, where male and female are the poles creating life anew.

From another perspective, there is the view, gleaned from the Tibetan Buddhist tradition, that maintains the idea of the individual is 'empty'. Moving over to the *Bhagavad Gita*, India's great scripture, the truth is that we are held perfectly in God. A God, it may be said, who conjures the odd cosmic flourish or who rests as pure potential. For us, a sign of the ebb of Self-amnesia is coming to a working acceptance of all material and worldly states that present themselves. It is far more desirable to be a buoyant and true manifestation of the One Life, where that life lives through you. It is an existence created by – made out of – pure love, a tableau, a show for itself, where 'everything' has its own renown. No burden but expression, magnificence and joy. The weight of the self is relieved – without taking drugs of oblivion or bunking off to a VR fantasy.

Money

Use and abuse

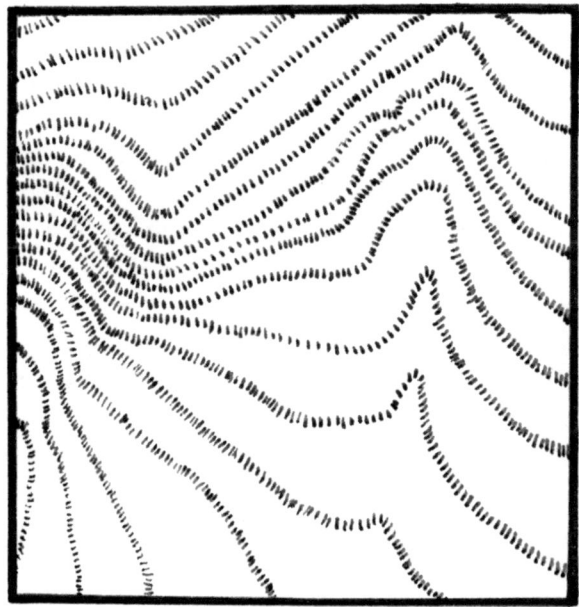

It is the love of money rather than money itself that is claimed to be the root of all evil. I am not sure this is the whole story, but whether in the red or the black an obsession with an entity we ourselves have created easily takes hold. True, money embodies command and opportunity. Nor do I deny the stature it may confer on an individual within a group (socially agreed). Nevertheless, I regard the status so derived as relatively primitive, and something from which we can choose to step away; a thing not in with the expansion of life becomes despised.

If money has captured us, though, then the story has a high chance of ending badly. This observation is accorded due deference, but it may be a wisdom that is only followed after it is not followed.

In Chaucer's *The Canterbury Tales*, *The Canon's Yeoman's Tale* and *The Pardoner's Tale* are splendid stories of some of the negative consequences. Somewhat farcical in the first, and chilling in the second, I commend them. In our own lives we are lucky to get away with just looking foolish. The big heist, however, has more of a dream quality to it in which to hide.

After signing up for the market, money is required to fuel it. Without the presence of money – in whatever form – we are back to the difficulties of matching demands in barter. However, deals of this type may be used to circumvent the problems of currency fluctuations. Conceivably, a planned economy could function without money, but it would be a special case.

In addition to being a medium of exchange, money serves as a store of value, subject to the level of inflation. Where it has no intrinsic value (a fiat currency), as is usually the case, it will still play the part, given agreement and trust. Ultimately, money could be categorised as a belief.

One can view it as a tool – to be used for either good or ill. Created/issued, for example, to develop and order an economy through tax obligations. Perhaps some of its allure may be explained by our daydreams of active laziness.

Then I take what I think is Derrick Jensen's point, which is since money is an abstract, rather than a concrete, entity, the gauging of 'enough' becomes difficult. Moreover, it may be argued that there is an element in human nature unable, from the beginning, to recognise sufficiency. (A rational response to endemic uncertainty?) This lack of limit, even if it is not labelled as pathological, can, unsurprisingly, lead to a crash. The tale of Icarus is more than story as entertainment.

Even in the absence of disaster – indeed whatever our financial state happens to be – we can find ourselves living in a world of abstraction, of number, and preoccupied with means rather than goals or desired conditions.

Following the establishment of money is the payment of interest on it. Usury has been condemned and understandably so. Certainly it does not display a thankfulness for one's blessings, and does not chime well with Galatians 6:2: 'Bear ye one another's burdens, and so fulfil the law of Christ.'

In a working economy however, as a charge for renting a resource, interest can be defended. Through investment, enterprise and the need to create may be realised. The rate is likely to include a premium for risk, and compensation for possible inflation. Savers receive interest payments for consumption foregone. There should be no exchequer levy on interest receipts as this would be double taxation.

A fee-based loan system could be another method. At all events the underlying forces are likely to be the same, presenting their demands in due course, in whatever name.

So interest facilitates flow, cycling, in an economy. Francis Bacon likened money to muck, it being no good unless spread. Bosch's wonderful painting, *Death and the Miser*, is cautionary. Miserliness, misery.

If one accepts the charging of interest there is still the question of whether rates are excessive. Intemperance in any form is a distortion, aesthetically an ugliness. It will be challenged eventually, especially from the deeper, energetic level. There is the contrast between a Credit Union and a loan shark.

Another accusation is that interest, particularly interest on the interest, stokes inequality. Attention, too, has been drawn to a greater rate of exploitation of resources taking place in order to pay back the loan. It is easy to see from the maths that there may never be enough money in existence for all debt to be cleared.

On the plus side, at policy level interest rates are useful in controlling inflationary pressures.

*

Internationally there are many currencies, which, in the absence of intervention, move automatically relative to one another, not only in response to fundamental economic conditions, but also to rumour and panic. This is where the currency speculators are found, working the system, feeding off market instability. The financial rewards for making the right call, for placing the right bet (for instance by selling short, i.e. selling high before one actually has ownership, with the intention of buying back at a lower price) can be enormous.

Successful players can then enter the real economy with their winnings, and secure steadier, more tangible assets. Speculators may be viewed as gamblers and parasites, with their activity pulling trade out of shape. However, they also perform a market correction function, curbing excessive highs and lows in price.

Much more pernicious in the markets are phenomena such as the predatory practice, on the part of the creditor, of using indebtedness to seize debtor assets. In an international setting this may form part of a strategy of economic imperialism. War, as military conflict, does not have to take place to achieve these goals.

Then there is cavalier trading by financial institutions, who are betting that any losses incurred, especially the largest ones, will be covered by others – by the taxpayer, or by society being deprived of public services into the future (government being anxious to preserve confidence in the financial system). 'Too big to fail' is the boast. It is a case of moral hazard. Neither is the State to steal from the people by not adjusting tax bands and allowances in accordance with inflation, or through, for that matter, taxation policies based on unproven anthropogenic climate change. A question always, always to be asked is on what, ultimately, prosperity is based. To the extent that a life is based on sin (to use that word), it amounts to less than nothing.

All these actions comprise a type of behaviour that plainly falls short, which 'misses the mark'. One wonders why there is not more opprobrium directed at these individuals (and companies and governments). Like Liberace they can continue to cry all the way to the bank, but a social signal – always potentially the precursor of something far more powerful – could be sent out. Avarice and a short memory go together, however.

*

Market price can overshoot in either direction. However, we expect that it will reflect, with time, the actual conditions found in the economy. Decisions based on underlying economic realities are predicted for the long-term. In the global economy, if a country is perceived as having, for example, a high social welfare provision, funded from taxation, then investment, first of all at the margin, will begin to go elsewhere. Higher costs affect competitiveness. And naturally, exchange rates reflect trading values. No State wishes to have the position of its currency on the slide.

Global lenders, too, can push up interest rates for a nation if they do not like the look of its community proposals.

World markets select for low priority in social expenditure, and generally for the lowest costs. This is a barrier to positive change. Analogously, Marx warned that socialism could only succeed in a key global coverage.

*

Sovereignty is trumped, as it is when corporations are, brazenly, given primacy in international trading agreements, and when the supranational bodies, the NGOs, managing these arrangements have no meaningful accountability. It is not free trade when rich countries impose tariffs on manufactures from poorer ones in order to protect their own industrial sectors. A less-developed country is kept to being just that, a resource provider, unable to add more value, and hence relatively poor. It is not free trade when industries receive subsidies for production, for example US cotton. You will find the game rigged; it is a way of doing business worthy of the smoothest crime family. Yet free trade itself can destabilise a native culture. A people will have to decide what material price they are prepared to pay to preserve a way of life. It is a dilemma.

A stronger element of self-sufficiency might be mooted, but this runs against comparative advantage in production. Furthermore, our daily needs predispose us to short-termism. On the other hand this may be the opportunity to instigate a more community-based economy, where human values are prioritised. True community entails gifts and reciprocity, relationships that are not monetised. Just as so much household work is not counted as economic activity. Also, humans can put soul into objects when making them, and this is picked up by others. The same applies to the delivery of services. A local currency will help to keep the money around.

And a parallel currency can challenge the banks' stranglehold. The market is good at responding with change where the benefits to producers and consumers of a good or service are poorly distributed.

A local economy necessarily is more devolved on individuals, most of whom, incidentally, have traditionally been belittled by an overbearing hegemony. We have an urgent need for de-conditioning, and for an awareness of this need in the first place. As they say, when you've been in the shithouse for so long you don't notice the stink.

In fact, one would find huge resources of latent talent, capability and motivation that, with the right guidance, would be more than equal to the task. Of more direct spiritual interest is that these are likely to create an environment where silence – taken from humanity by overwhelming industrialisation – makes a comeback. I also expect alienation from both natural rhythms and groupings to be rolled back.

The question of national security comes up. Greater economic independence enhances it in one way but may jeopardise it in another if GNP (gross national product) is not sufficient to provide a credible framework of self-defence. Expansionist régimes, possessing a hefty military to further their interests, must be watched. International power imbalances have the potential to give rise to political blackmail or indeed armed attack on weak or invented pretexts. The natural reflex is to keep in some kind of step with the world so as to head-off these hazards. It is another facet of the tendency towards homogeneity. Equally though, among nations, mutual interest and longer-term prospects need to be stressed (for example, in avoiding the ruinous expense of a perpetual arms race). An opponent may not conquer you but can cause serious damage. Besides, a third party, the tertius gaudens, can always slip in to take advantage of you both in your impaired states. In *12 Rules for Life: An Antidote to Chaos*, Jordan B. Peterson is talking about lobsters, but the scene transfers. In the end, as W.H. Auden puts it, 'We must love one another or die'.

Every autumn I see, in our little orchard, the alpha blackbird use a large amount of energy chasing away his fellows from the fallen fruit when there is more than enough for everyone. It is a melancholy parable.

To come back to money itself, and also to conclude. In promulgating economic fairness – something instinctively understood – money may conceivably begin to lose just a little of its glamour. Economics, after all, is a notoriously unglamorous subject. It has to do with facilitation; savour lies within the human experience. Money, like happiness, is best regarded as a consequence. An understanding of the drivers at work cuts through the complexity multiplying in the markets, including all the financial products available. Really there is surprisingly little to say about money. We can take the trance and the aggression out of it though, if we wish. If Shakespeare is essentially correct in observing that 'All the world's a stage' – for me more a pantomime – then it is folly to fight over possessing mere props and scenery.

Stuff

The freedom of enough

As might be gathered from the title of this chapter the focus is not going to be on the furnishing of necessities, the basics of human survival. These markets have a logic of their own, although the distinction between 'necessities' and 'luxuries' in a contemporary consumer society is going to be somewhat vague. Rather it will take its cue from the poet Ovid's 'amor sceleratus habendi' – the accursed love of possessing.

Parenthetically, having power over the supply of essentials is a very effective method of political and social control, although not without the risk of it blowing up in serious popular revolt. It is one half of the Roman 'bread and circuses', deemed necessary to keep the citizenry quiet.

I will be concentrating on the consumerist side, where ever-increasing buying has a set of negative ramifications. Principally, on when it has become a ruinous creed, fuelled by advertisers creating dissatisfaction. (When does their product fantasy become fraud?) It is a self-sustaining system when business sells us products and services designed to ameliorate negative effects coming from those things we have already bought from it. A mass production economy can so easily fill up the place with a mixture of the drab and the tawdry. One of Orwell's themes is about 'sham'. It is easy to read our own times in his 1939 *Coming Up for Air*. Running alongside there is much personal isolation in the contemporary work-and-buy society. I have a friend, a Samaritans volunteer, who tells me that unwanted aloneness is big amongst callers. The character of the economy cannot be entirely to blame but the contractual obligations of the market always threaten to edge out courtesy in human interaction. D.H. Lawrence had already railed against the middle-class existence; someone had to write 'How Beastly The Bourgeois Is'. There is a debate here that needs to be had by each age in its own language.

As a group we have gone down the road of increased consumption instead of downsizing for a more balanced way of being. Even here ownership must be set against hire availability, liquidity contingency and the freedom of tastes to change. The personality has, again and again, foregone cherished projects. Sadly, the moment passes and retirement is typically too late. Apologies for the stereotyping but I do not immediately associate a Harley-Davidson thrumming on the drive with a pebbledash maisonette and Scottie dog.

Whatever image it takes to wake us up.

Acquiring goods and services is now even more of a method of building an identity. The result usually earns a respect of sorts, even if it is only grudging. Possessions send out an emphatic signal, and it is one of impressive immediacy. Materialism is triumphant, but envy and mockery inevitably lurk. The successful person, splashing it about, may be regarded as a vulgar arriviste, or as someone whose clothes wear them, for instance. The nouveau riche probably wishes to move in new circles, but in unfamiliar settings social cues are going to be missed. Accents will be ridiculed, and all work and no play may have made Jack a dull boy. Peas may be eaten off the knife, or sips taken from a fingerbowl. The only elegance is that of a pantomime horse. How *frightful* – that's the word. The hapless person becomes the butt of stock humour. See Molière's play, *Le Bourgeois gentilhomme*. The historic sumptuary laws, where you were compelled to dress according to your class, may have gone but it is left to the next generation to possess the manners and proper taste, to become 'one of us'!

What I take from critical theorist Herbert Marcuse is the idea of the individual 'stupefied' by the ready availability of consumer satisfaction.

Also, where consumption is concerned, that basic of economics – diminishing marginal utility – soon kicks in. This is the decreasing benefit accrued from each additional unit of the item used. If the primary characteristics of life are survival and reproduction then pleasure will play no more than a supporting part. In evolutionary thinking the ability to receive a surfeit of pleasure will not be selected for. Sensualism and gratification must be limited both in their duration and to what they adhere. Hence, natural restrictions are placed on hedonism. From another perspective the spirit is not to languish. Either way, we are kept moving, and a faculty for boredom redirects. So consuming soon hits a wall.

There may be feelings of anger and dismay when things

do not hit the spot any longer, especially when the story sold to us from childhood (a promise even) was that they would. This expectation lies at the heart of the 'American Dream'. But I think Washington, Jefferson and Franklin were aiming somewhat higher. The United States of America is altogether a cautionary tale.

There is poverty in the midst of plenty. Nevertheless, we do not give up, but procure more goodies, or off-the-shelf experiences, in order to shore up the situation.

This is the beginning of the well-known slippery slope, and it sometimes ends in real degradation, particularly if the financing comes from credit. The ego operating outside of its limited area of legitimacy leads to our undoing and us missing the 'glory of God'. Bad debt punches holes in the economy too. There is some defence for spirited consumption when it is an exploration of identity, or a stunt opposing stultifying bourgeois values. However, *au fond,* to splurge and binge is not the path out of suffering, as the hunger is for realities of a different quality altogether. It has been postulated that both the taking of sunshine on the body and an intake of sweet foods act as substitutes for human love. The greater message is that I am already of worth beyond calculation, and that I have always been loved. I am more than all the categories in which I have been placed. I am also all the things I am no good at, or do not know or possess. And I don't want anyone else's life. I need not *deserve* every last bit of love but the teaching remains, from Mathew 6:20, to 'lay up for yourselves treasures in heaven'. It is difficult for the world to contain us but the trick is to participate in the economy on a soul basis.

Was it Lenin who wanted toilets to be made of gold?

I look to a move of health resources into assisting people with existential crisis and into helping clear emotional mess – things once performed by more intimate community. To prevent, for example, the path from woundedness to nihilism being taken. It would also be good to have you not turn on those closest to you when they fail to rescue you from the human condition, or on those whose other views of the world you perceive as threats to your very identity. These are other fields of hygiene, and will be patient-centred of course. So much of life involves disentangling early experiences, both good and bad. A balance in healthcare between proactive and reactive makes good economic sense too.

Acquisitiveness builds up walls around the person. In this state one becomes as remote as when being observed through the wrong end of a telescope. The end-point of consumerism is the delusion that we can choreograph the rest of our lives. It also exemplifies locating the source of lasting welfare in the external and the uncertain. The project is, in any case, flawed as in grasping at pleasures we get in their way or even nullify them altogether. On the other hand, in attempting to avoid pain one fuses with the idea of it, this looming in awareness, with perhaps more layers of anxiety built upon it. The skill is in dancing with the two partners.

There is the possibility for real individual change as the personal misery increases – from some type of revelation or simply by reason of being compelled to think – but no guarantee that it will be made. There are casualties. The parallel with drug addiction is obvious.

One impediment will be when an individual identifies with decline, seeing, from egocentricity, a pathos in his or her 'fate'. Consumption can also seek the ornate – with aesthetics becoming ethics – alongside the ennui-driven infliction of garish novelty on oneself. This is interesting but phoney; the reality is so much ersatz. To quote Cervantes: 'Hunger is the best sauce in the world.' Consumerism tends to shift from objective good to subjective indulgence. This is seen in what people choose to eat, with gross satisfaction displacing nutritional needs. Industrial capitalism had already cut corners in workers' diets.

Still, I will defend our human ways where Christmas, for

example, is concerned. This time of the year is better seen simply as an occasion for a mid-winter feast (a statement that we are very much still here) and a celebration of the return of the light. These are material responses to material circumstances. As for having Jesus' birth on 25 December, it is part of a hostile takeover bid by the new religion for the old.

However, we get the presents thing wrong. The gold, frankincense and myrrh of the nativity were about reverent recognition and devotion. They were not rote frippery. And when the Christmas lights go up in October, or even earlier, one must diagnose a famished and drifting spirit.

Along with the personal gorging (the term is intended to be descriptive rather than condemnatory) is the standing amongst others created by a more rarefied expenditure – on prestigious articles. Something of this has already been mentioned. Humans, it appears, will always jockey for position, and statements are there to be made, both about one's power and, more ambitiously, about one's taste, one's 'class'. Higher demand with a higher price may be seen. This occurs with the so-called Veblen goods, named after US economist Thorstein Veblen, the creator of the theory of 'conspicuous consumption'. However, they are often much underutilised – think of yachts in marinas. That may be part of the point.

Some lines from Alexander Pope (1688–1744) express the surge of vanity when it comes to property:

'At Timon's villa let us pass a day,
Where all cry out, What sums are thrown away!
So proud, so grand, of that stupendous air,
Soft and Agreeable come never there.
Greatness, with Timon, dwells in such a draught
As brings all Brobdignag before your thought.
To compass this, his building is a town,
His pond an ocean, his parterre a down:
Who must but laugh, the Master when he sees,

A puny insect, shiv'ring at a breeze!
Lo, what huge heaps of littleness around!
The whole, a laboured quarry above ground.'

This is display behaviour. To be a little crude, it is a big dick being waved about. Not much has changed. Being passionate about these matters can, I admit, conduct one into the territory of stony-faced, Victorian pronouncements. I have no wish to stifle vigour, exuberance or even a kind of madness – economics cannot always be the final arbiter. We need expressions of our values, and to make statements about what defines us. In John 12:3 Mary Magdalene anoints the feet of Jesus with a pricey ointment.

However, majoring in this type of action becomes distasteful in a world where so many still cannot even meet fundamental needs, let alone give their lives a fair chance. It is depressing that there are so many goods and services catering for the hard-hearted. These are the markets for self-love's adornments. Purchases have, in context, their own shame measured out in them. To no surprise their design can mirror the defining attitude of these customers. I found myself in a BMW showroom recently. The cars at the upper end of the range did catch the eye. Taking a stand against the bland is good; no problem there. Yet the front of one – the swooping curves of the bonnet, sharp grille and narrowed headlights – was typical. The manufacturer may cite aerodynamics but it was the visage of a pitiless predator. Of course it was in a gaudy and all-taking black.

Status goods, indeed, depend on other people not having them. They embody an attitude we would condemn in others. A spiritual danger for the wealthy is them calculating that they can afford their own bad manners. I believe most of us are highly attuned socially. No doubt this is part of our evolutionary inheritance. So what drives a person will, sooner or later, be picked up by others. Relationships may be at risk or become less rich. Furthermore, in time, one's outer being will tend to mirror one's inner nature. You get a 'look'. In Islamic tradition, there is the race of the Jinn. The benevolent of them have a transfixing beauty, while the malevolent ones present as vile and horrifying. It would be interesting to see how, for instance, a group of children drew an individual who had devoted years to personal aggrandisement. The youngest of us tend to have a fresh perception and a refreshing candour.

The parade of self-importance can become heightened, possibly eliciting widespread disgust. Even in Native American culture there were the Potlatch ceremonies, occasions of competitive gift-giving, and, in the extreme, of ostentatious destruction of value. I have a memory of some character lighting a cigar with a high denomination note or bill, which sounds like a scene in a film. Then there is the City high-roller flushing the toilet with champagne (urban myth?). These acts say that I am rich enough to destroy my own wealth. They lean, though, more towards the silly than the wicked. Indeed, there is a strand of humour relying on the breaking of taboos. And human beings do need to test where the boundaries lie, even if only through posture. Sometimes the icons get smashed.

In consumer choice there is a desire to either stand out in mass society or indicate a belonging to it by a show of loyalty. An attempt to reconcile these opposing forces may be witnessed in a single purchase. One might also propose a form of enantiodromia at work, which is the course where one thing is succeeded by its opposite. Punk drainpipes did follow those Prog Rock flares. Fashions do, and must, go on forever.

Couture and coiffure help to offset the simply awful decay of the body. Not to be over-groomed, like some river-boat gambler, but enough to hold onto some swagger. At my age you can't do scruffy. I do not wish to look as if I live in a caravan in a field.

*

Philosopher José Ortega y Gasset remarked that 'to live as one likes is plebeian; the noble man aspires to order and law'. I appreciate the thrust of this statement, but I am not entirely comfortable with its form. Before using the term 'plebeian' with such loathing, consideration should be given to the conditions that have been typically present for this class – brutalising occupations, scant pay, unpredictable income, poor housing and diet, lack of respect from wider society, depressed expectations, harsh choices, the necessity to take whatever opportunities that come along, and so on. In fact, being in an altogether weak economic position means that you have to be rich to be poor. The song, 'Walk A Mile In My Shoes', addresses the dismissive those who do not know. One has to question why such a marked social stratification has not only been allowed to develop, but also to persist. Do not expect the will to life to be anything other than uncompromising. How many elderly or disabled people would *you* find yourself elbowing out of the way or treading on in order to get to the lifeboats? I do, however, take the point of the undesirability – for anyone – of allowing existence to remain centred in the 'lower self', which is the place of compulsions and caprice.

Persistent indigence lays waste to the personality, shutting most of it off. Getting out of poverty also requires rehabilitation of the poverty mind, so that the person can see possibilities once more.

The Roman satirist Juvenal is typically devastating when he observes: 'The misfortunes of poverty carry with them nothing harder to bear than that it makes men ridiculous.'

At the upper end of the riches scale an individual may be more a caretaker of that prosperity, serving an uncertain future at the expense of that most valuable of times, the present. In effect a wealth fund manager. If life can be distilled to relationship, then it is not much of one with something that is not alive. Alternatively, where consumption is not deferred, the person might be discovered wandering between sofa and swimming pool, already intoxicated. A Sybarite. So many diversions, so little direction. (Watch Fellini's *La Dolce Vita* for the fun-less antics of the party scene.) A unique and potent personality is kept from being born. One remains curled up – reminiscent of the hands of battlefield corpses. If this book had a sound-track this is where 'Lush Life', sung by the fabulous Sarah Vaughan, would be played. Likewise, in the form of your entourage you might have created a monster, something not too dissimilar to Bacchus' train in Titian's *Bacchus and Ariadne*.

The children become frightened when the adults stop being adults. Hedonism's shadow is grief.

It is sobering to think that if we were in sole charge of our lives they would be, most probably, disasters. Our desire to do deals with God makes us not see. To be a person of substance is hard-won. Concern yourself with being able to love, avoid becoming a collector of grievances. Anyway, if a being is dependent on an environment then where are the bounds of the real self?

The ordinary mind is a glut of wanting and fearing, its agitation energy-devouring. It recalls a cheap cocktail – sticky, bitter, a display of trash colour. The beginning of ending unnecessary suffering is choking off the stream of actions stemming from a misrepresenting self-conception. Throughout everything, though, the spirit is never a victim.

To be clamped to the material side of life is to be out of balance, and to be robbed of poise, although I do sympathise with the incarnated where this is a pathetic attempt to summon a simulacrum of our origin. It is limitation, giving rise to a background malaise on account of one not stepping into the full flow of prana. Peace, the state of spirit, does not come. Therefore we are exiled from our complementary consciousness, incomplete, in a body not yet spiritualised. Instead, there is a smiling detachment to be had. It is better to walk through the world of objects with some serenity, inhabiting yourself, and to allow possessions to pass peacefully through your hands. Things are more beautiful because they do not last for ever.

A person may need the reorientation of a breakdown.

Moreover, just a few quid directed elsewhere could bring so much benefit. It might even turn out to be transformative. This is diminishing marginal utility in operation again, but moving in the opposite direction. Progressive taxation, again, is arguably a justified recourse. Charitable donation, as a social reflex, would also assist in restoring some balance. I wish us to understand the sheer privilege of giving.

Look for the larger picture. Freedom is messy, but this is no reason for its restriction. Freedom is the point – messiness a small price.

There is the Spike Milligan quip: 'Money can't buy you happiness but it does bring you a more pleasant form of misery.' Money in the bank and a portfolio of other assets do confer room to manoeuvre. They provide, too, some insurance in a world of swirling change. Lives are, as a consequence, considerably less stressful. I would go so far as to recommend subventions as an alternative to medical treatment, when more direct intervention is not indicated. The body's wisdom is given room.

The contrast, to be in a position of minimal control for most of the time, and to be unable to mount an effective response to events, is substantial stress, and attritional to the psyche. Not easily grasped by the monied, this is a real feature of poverty; the fight-or-flight mechanism is of little use here. One simply waits to be overwhelmed.

Part of the answer – platitudinous I know – is remembering that strength comes from being able to act out of unity. This is the *raison d'être* of a trade union. A symbol is the fasces, the rods bundled together. (Unfortunately this has come to be associated with murderous tyrannies.) An understood togetherness is a great protection for everyone, not least psychologically. It also encourages fairness. To back up the inherent sense of what is fair, current judgements of what is acceptable with respect to a whole range of issues could be made plain, as statistics, by standard market research practice. This would side-step accusations of unhelpful subjectivity.

Considering accepted norms, it is interesting to see what forms ridicule or shaming take. It can be rough. There is the skimmington from Thomas Hardy's *The Mayor of Casterbridge*. It can go from being sent to Coventry, to outright intimidation, even physical violence. The potential impact on social animals should not be underestimated.

These are occurrences of human groupings seeking a minimal state of stability, and may be viewed as an adjunct to a legal system. Also, in lieu of an initiation rite, banter and joking are able to convey to members that none is above the group.

Societies operate by carrot and stick. Adoption of Natural Law may not get rid of the need for sanctions, but will direct us to something more elevated than equivalents of the rewards and punishments given to lab rats.

I wonder if a mathematical equation has been produced expressing the relationship between the level of income / wealth inequality and social unrest / revolution. Simplistic on its own, yet it may possess predictive power in context. Chaos might be averted by an equivalent of the Jewish Jubilee, which attended to economic extremes resulting over time. Taking place every fiftieth year, it included the cancelling of debts.

Where there is a dearth of practical wisdom, by being estranged from the beneficial side of tradition, all the unlearned lessons of history return. The smoke rises above the city, sirens are screaming, and they might get through the gates this time. Then just watch the fury and destruction. Terrifying scenarios, with many innocents caught up in the havoc. Nor will the zillionaires' patrolled estates, private islands and panic rooms save them. They will be dragged from these. The more studied retribution will come later.

The warnings will have been there, analogous to the developing symptoms of an illness – both ignored at great peril. Society can only be functioning horribly inefficiently, with significant resources needing to be devoted to propping things up. Nothing like 'the greatest happiness of the greatest number' is being realised.

The *Tao Tê Ching* puts it:

'When bronze and jade fill your hall

It can no longer be guarded.'

To not wish to know anything about a developing underclass, beyond a few contemptuous jokes, is an attitude courting disaster.

*

Summing up, I am in accord with the view that, outside of reasonable variation, the taking of more than one needs is a stealing from the world. It is hoarding and stagnation rather than flow, which surely characterises life as we understand it. We have only made the prison a little more comfortable. One has to grow from craver into appreciator, otherwise the karma of clutter pulls the possessor down.

By contrast spiritual 'goods' are always somehow new.

I think medieval theologian Meister Eckhart said something like for a person to say 'thank you', just once, was enough. What is always open to us is to allow gratitude and generosity to come. This may happen from events in the world, or through letting the mind have stillness. Our own lives are a gift; handing it on is to be aligned spiritually. This may be as acknowledgement and listening, or in practical assistance. When deliberation is needed, let it not be awkward. To use the idiom of Piero Ferrucci, teacher of psychosynthesis, one's life can be one's masterpiece. What consumer item compares with this? Why neglect your greatest asset?

We can attain a greatness. Or be something like a flower opening for ever. We also build, through loving God (as the universal life principle), a spiritual bond, a life with the Sacred. The Andante from Hummel's 'Concerto in E flat Major' for trumpet and orchestra, in my hearing at least, identifies these. Healing, of course, means to become whole. Proverbs has it:

'Where there is no vision, the people perish.'

Where there is, everything else follows.

The Political Settlement

High democracy and enlightenment

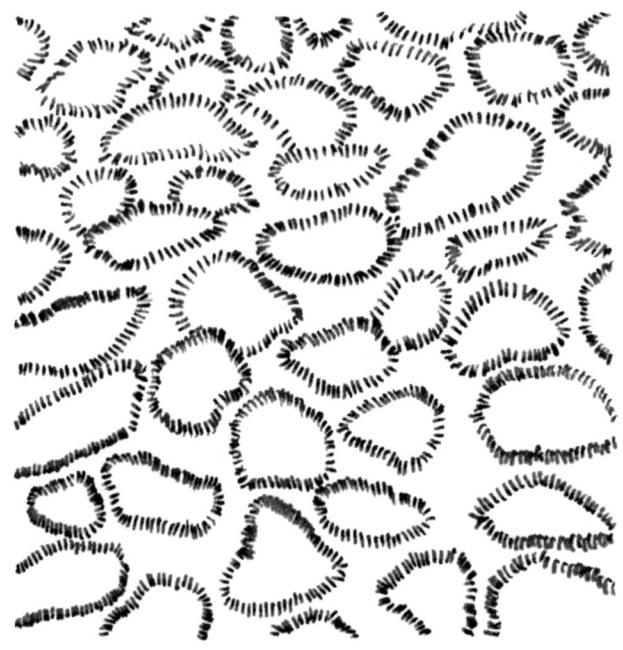

There will have to be a broad impetus, followed by a mandate, in order to evolve the economy, or have it jump to the position of sanity and fairness. The predominant concern will not be about simply growing it, that given of the past.

When it comes to public opinion we might look back at history and agree on the need for an equivalent of a Marxist-Leninist 'vanguard party', there to galvanise the people. Not the 'dictatorship of the proletariat' then. Lenin made a very interesting remark: 'The history of all countries shows that the working class exclusively by its own efforts is able to develop only trade union consciousness.' It must be questioned whether the new revolutionaries, like the old rulers, only wish to herd and corral the populace, and create yet another oligarchy.

Genuine leadership will have a place, but not mass coercion. In any case, without popular support, fresh government could not endure. Manipulation – in all its guises – is by definition more cloaked, but will fall in the end, given its basis in falsehood. There is the not unimportant matter of when, but the Tao and its power cannot be hidden from.

Actually, a couple of the qualities I see as necessary for leaders / representatives to possess is love – yes, love – for the people, and an expansive soul resilient to despair, however these may be judged. Embracing the concept of the servant-king will help counter the megalomania rush upon entering office.

As ever, the opponents, like goblins watching you as you take the path through the woods, will need to be reckoned with. Their goal will be to neutralise any new initiatives. Powerful worldly interests are suspicious of any alteration in the ways things are done anyway. They usually just sit there, grimly, or in magnificent self-justification. In reality, for a clique to retain a position of immoderate privilege, any sincere democracy must be subverted. The English Civil War sparked debates on the Parliamentarian side about what would follow the monarchy. A recurring theme, though, was the grandees' fear of an extended franchise; it was thought that the poorer would then wish to redistribute the wealth of the rich amongst themselves. Was this the real reason behind the property qualification for voting? Whatever, a rare opportunity to begin a new world passed and the radicals were suppressed.

In any case, Power will seep into organisations for change and corrupt them. This is part of an historical cycle. Generally money finds a way in, sufficiently even to fashion a pretend democracy.

'The world is governed by very different personages from what is imagined by those who are not behind the scenes.' Disraeli.

Sadly, we appear habituated to – and passive in the face of – a wealthy, self-proclaimed élite controlling key institutions. It can be right there in our faces. We may even find ourselves applauding them – whilst being suckered into fighting amongst each other. Actions undertaken by this minority, ostensibly for the common good, are likely to be either forms of window-dressing or sops. Their influence radiates downwards. Reminiscent of the dynamic in a primate troupe, it pervades the whole of society. It is like the lettering running through a stick of rock. Egalitarian change is confronted by a formidable pyramid of threats and kickbacks. In addition, the dead-wood and flummery of the Establishment will continue to accumulate until the people come to their senses.

Add to this mind control, a subject worth studying in its own right. To keep, in a modern society, 'the great unwashed' in its place, there will have to be 'engineering of consent' and techniques of mass persuasion. The adaption of religious phraseology and archetypal images from the psyche to this end is particularly interesting. Everything will be weaponised, I am sorry to say. The aim – for the patricians – is victory without having to fight. However, these intrigues (mostly implemented by a regiment of stooges) effectively cheat people of their lives, and their dignity before God.

Of particular relevance to this book are the applications of mind-control techniques to productivity and industrial relations, in order to screw more out of the workforce. Also to have the public accept the system as it stands. The years go by and they're the same!

Those movements dissatisfied with the status quo must expect their positions and proposals to be misrepresented – or ignored – by a corporately-controlled media (them again). Moreover, they must anticipate the infiltration, and the harassment of their members. An effective challenge to power comes with a health warning. You might even be found face down floating in the river. Another nightmare is when authority asserts disagreement to be mental illness, resulting in the forcible detention and 'treatment' of the individual – with zombie meds and the excision of 'false beliefs'.

The irony is that our own figure of justice is blindfolded, symbolising equal dispensation to all, regardless of rank. If standards do slip the rogues quickly take over.

From these circumstances one might understand this passage from Matthew (10:34) a little more clearly: 'Think not that I am come to send peace on earth: I came not to send peace, but a sword.'

I took the primary duty of government to be the protection of the persons who elected it (together with those who voted otherwise). Unfortunately, the reality is that this is not a priority. Rather, more sectional concerns win out – repeatedly. There are, after all, the campaign donations, the 'revolving door' between industry and governmental departments, and companies' threats to hold back investment if they cannot get regulations watered down. I may not be surprised at this, but am always disappointed. The greatest enemy of the State turns out to be its people – and vice versa. At worst a country becomes merely a business run by a small group for its own ends. Pride and patriotism are cynically fashioned and then put to work. It is a fake nation, best serviced by compromised and therefore blackmailable politicians. Extreme wealth is likely to engender disdain and delusion in its holders.

Authority structures are also very good at serving themselves, demoting, over time, their public service reason for being.

*

A good example, currently, of contempt for the greater good is seen in the extraordinary proliferation of wireless communications. Not least it is a marketing phenomenon, and I will spend some time on the technology as a product as it affects so much else. Wi-Fi is one system using energy of a frequency and nature to which humans are not evolutionarily adapted. The radiation is classified by the World Health Organisation as a potential (2B) carcinogen, and it is also linked to, inter alia, cardiovascular diseases, male infertility and behavioural problems. Long-term effects are not yet known; therefore we are the guinea pigs. Is this the biggest experiment in human history? I am not aware that the population has given its considered, express consent. A case of breaching the Nuremberg Code, 1947? Interestingly, a new drug would simply not get approval for the market in the way wireless systems have been let loose.

Furthermore, use of this technology adds to the total load of 'electrosmog' from this band already present – from DECT cordless 'phones, and mobile 'phones and masts, for example. Then we are looking at the mass installation of (so-called) Smart Meters, which will irradiate us in our own homes 24/7. Not forgetting, too, the attack from space coming from a swarm of satellites. Dr Erica Mallery-Blythe states that EMFs (electromagnetic fields) are in the order of a quintillion – that is a one with eighteen zeros after it – times higher than natural background levels.

Is the information readily available to consumers, employees, parents, students, etc. so that each may make an informed choice? I see little evidence that it is. It may be a situation of an invalid contract; an agreement is void if there has not been full disclosure of terms. Moreover, in public spaces there is no option for avoidance, which is an issue of human rights as well.

I know of four studies that associate this frequency with impaired cognition, and two with impaired memory. Heightened activation of the Central Nervous System (CNS), leading to its dysregulation? Displacement of natural frequencies at the cellular level by a disruptive resonance? So as to putting Wi-Fi into schools, colleges and universities, does anyone get the awful irony? Safer, wired alternatives exist of course. A review in *The Lancet* from December 2018 of 2,000+ peer-reviewed studies on the impact of wireless technology on human and animal systems showed that 68.2 per cent found significant biological effects. It concluded: 'This weight of scientific evidence refutes the prominent claim that the deployment of wireless technologies poses no health risks at the currently permitted non-thermal radio-frequency exposure levels.' The purveyors of official limits could and should be arraigned, both individually and corporately. Beginning with a charge of criminal negligence? A recent paper by Rubik et al., *Evidence for a Connection between COVID-19 and Exposure to Radiofrequency Radiation from Wireless Telecommunications Including Microwaves and Millimeter Waves*, OSF Preprints, 2021, is no surprise. To quote: 'In short, wireless communication radiation is a ubiquitous environmental stressor, and evidence presented here suggests that it is a contributing factor in the COVID-19 pandemic.'

What kind of culture, or 'democracy', permits the overriding of public health by corporate profits and government tax revenues? A denatured world is produced, in which all life forms are assaulted. Not smart. Yes, the truth is unpalatable. It seems to me that we inconvenient humans must also be made to fit the technology, as per the bed of Procrustes.

Perhaps humanness is regarded as inferior to the machine. There are not many spiritual errors greater than this. On the consumer side, it is clear that many people, in order to be 'in-group' members, are willing to risk or trade their own health, a little like Esau, for a mess of pottage.

My understanding from the work of Allan Frey is that there is a possibility of even a very weak EMF signal untuning the normal function of a living being. That is a finding to be buried in an information war.

Reflecting on Bonhoeffer's Theory of Stupidity the denial has to be, at its root, a moral problem and not one of intelligence. Certainly the slovenly and the wasteful are discovered in the very concept of wireless coverage, which is shriekingly self-centred too, not unlike carpeting the world instead of finding a good pair of shoes.

Historian Yuval Harari says that 'the greatest industry of the twenty-first century will probably be to *upgrade* human beings' (my italics). The dangers are obvious. In its striving, humanity cancels itself, completing the tragedy.

*

It is always wise to put the 'cui bono?' ('who benefits?') question. Even in the absence of specific conspiracy, a subject strangely taboo (theories are meant to be tested, y'know), it has to be in the masters' interests to have the populace a little dulled, with the edge taken off the natural ebullience of life. Yet not so much that these people are not still useful or productive. It is another illustration of the deep wrong of treating individuals as means instead of ends in themselves. And if the masses actually pay for their enslavement, *tant mieux*.

How many know that a Wi-Fi field can be used to create an image of the space where it is present? You are offering to be spied on.

More malign is that undermining, by MW (microwave)

exposure, of human fertility – female in addition to male. I am not pointing the finger but this is obviously a force in lowering the population in the longer term. Since the incursion of this radiation is not checked with any seriousness by the authorities, speculation as to why there is this inaction is inevitable.

Supplementary to the health consequences is the question of our ability to frame thought – effectively and efficiently – if linked constantly to communication and information devices. Does a superficial processing of data take precedence over deeper judgements that need time? Are we even addressing the right questions? Also, is there an effect on the richness of social relations when human interaction is dominated by screen and text? Not a good prospect emotionally, one would think, for beings already starved of touch.

Let the hypotheses be tested.

It is not difficult to market this and other wireless communication formats as indispensable, great, sexy, cool or whatever. Psychology, as a discipline, has been both used and abused. But I do not deny that buyers bear responsibility too, especially before an addiction to convenience sets in. Or an amnesia over how life was actually possible before these gizmos arrived. The question posed in Katie Singer's *An Electronic Silent Spring* (2014) is whether to have more technology or to live within biological limitations. Cost-benefit analysis is useful in reaching economic decisions, but some things really should not be part of a bargain. Innovation will tend to lead to life in society consisting of a series of discontinuities that occur at increasing frequency.

My feeling is that the real powers, sorry to say, not only deride, but verily despise, the hoi polloi. The second are to be 'farmed' by the first. In striving for objectives governments have a record of throwing sections of the populace to the wolves. Authority may seek to justify this by utilitarian calculation or from a definition of usefulness. Without taking a personal moral stance in the face of such actions, it might be you who is sacrificed tomorrow for some other goal.

Pace hinders establishment of perspective and the mad momentum does not slacken. The introduction of 5G looms. This has to do more with the wider environment and network infrastructure, though there is not much 'outer' or 'inner' with a penetrative technology. To add to the sheer intensity of this bioactive pollution, 100 per cent of the land may already have been prepared for coverage – exceptions are seen as defects. This is more than an invasion; it is another face of totalitarianism. Those most physically vulnerable to this miasma will have basic human rights stripped away from them. As for the rest of the population, I see them becoming more and more like sickly machine hybrids leading 'lives' of limited personal meaning. A sci-fi nightmare? Probably not as lurid, but stealth and increment could head in the direction of a Luciferian freak show.

To discount the plight of the most affected is foolish – much like muzzling the guard dogs, or the coal miner ignoring the dead canary at the bottom of its cage. The corollary of (aggressive) certainty happens to be cruelty, here satisfied to see the afflicted remain refugees in their own country.

Machines move us out of being present with ourselves, disrupting personal coherence. This on top of the fact that it is difficult for us to access our true nature. Time spent trammelled by technology can be seen as dead time. If being is a chord that is struck, how much is actually ringing out in us now?

Employing a machine to locate ourselves collapses sense of place; multichannel perception is not exercised by us. 'Use it or lose it.' Falling back before computational intelligence means our diminution.

It is clear that the more digital connectivity there is the more passes one will have to have in order to navigate the system. Human agency will be removed at most levels. That is the warning.

5G is also bad news for trees. Research from the University of Surrey indicates mast heights at tree level as having a lowered reach and reliability. I expect the powers pushing the project to act in two ways. First, by taking out trees as a fait accompli, and second, by coming up with all sorts of spurious reasons as to why they had to go. If trees lock up carbon, don't we need more of them? They are also very much companion beings for us on this planet, not just with the O2/CO2 exchange. To raise the rate of their destruction shows how wanton and alienated are those who insist how societies should be. Aliens are already here. They live amongst us, they look like us. There are indeed occasions for lawful rebellion.

It may well be that the 5G project will only begin to be reversed when governments are confronted with increasing health costs (from treating a sicker populace) combined with a decreasing tax revenue from a less productive workforce. However, we are still in the exponential increase section of the trajectory. A fast buck will be made before any investigations take place, then there are the prepared excuses to fall back on.

Adding to the grave weakening of health, and therefore of the quality of life, this latest wave of commercially-engendered pollution follows the 100,000, approximately, novel chemicals already present in the environment. Most of them have not been adequately tested. Further, the potential for synergistic effects from them operating in combination creates an unmanageable complexity for effective understanding. (Applied science also 'dabbles in the occult'.) Their cavalier use is reckless and wrecking. The world is treated little better than an overflowing dustbin, and leaves unknown others from the future to deal with the mess. Dr Dominique Belpomme, President of ARTAC (Association for Research on Treatment Against Cancer), states that 80–90 per cent of cancers are linked to the environment. The excursion into nuclear power, as well as being economically questionable, creates a hostage to fortune, as we have seen. The same holds for the hopelessly ignorant genetic modification of food. This is not harmony, just hubris. I think it was Dr Rosalie Bertell who believed the likely fate of humankind to be extinction by poisoning.

This carry-on does not amount to stewardship of the planet, and we miss the opportunity to be co-creators.

By its preponderance, wireless technology has become the norm, and therefore, by dubious reasoning, something we must live with happily. I have already alluded to a dependence, that profiteerer's dream, brought about in the user. Part of that though, to be honest, has come from the restructuring of working and other arrangements.

With the amount of money at stake it would be surprising for voices of doubt and protest to be treated any other way than ruthlessly. A market has become rapidly integral, and it is booming. For the State, other advantages are an enhanced surveillance capability and control potential due to the public's use of the networks.

As for indication of harm, agencies tasked with regulation may look in the wrong place. If this is intentional, in subservience to the potentates, then at least plausibility can be presented by an 'investigation'. Where the wireless phenomenon is concerned, there is little doubt that the Precautionary Principle, to which the UK has signed up, is being ignored. Use of carefully crafted, legalistic phraseology adds to the evasiveness. Regarding Wi-Fi, the UK Government's Health Protection Agency claimed that there is 'no consistent evidence' of ill-health in the 'general' population. For practical purposes this is a statement approaching meaninglessness. Wretches such as these are also wont to fall into the (accustomed) logical error of equating 'absence of evidence' with 'evidence of absence'. Specious reassurance is their line, but it comes from painful intellectual gymnastics.

*

Other elements of the malaise affecting the official body supposedly there to protect public health in this area include the use of outdated evidence, the employment of man of straw arguments, and the failure to appoint, in an advisory capacity, any physician who actually treats the victims. Nevertheless, we are told what a great job it is doing. It may even have some funky new logo, and a mission statement of insulting vacuity.

Corruption? Conflict of interest? Incompetence? Mental inertia? The truth may even include an element of Orwellian double-think. I would be looking for a charge of misprision. Add complicity in Ecocide too. Whatever other elements of the profile, the organisation is still an outgrowth of exploitative thought and action.

A parallel to the pass wireless technology has received is the extraordinary status conferred, in medicine, on vaccines. Authorities have founded their policies with respect to both on data sets known to be inadequate. Will someone show me the routine, randomised, placebo-controlled, double-blind tests for any regular (childhood) vaccination, on which a licence needs to be based? The retrospective, if not prospective, epidemiology, which includes the all-important Vaccinated vs. Unvaccinated (VU) studies? Where are they? What we have is not the vaunted 'evidence-based medicine', but a dreadful example of irrationality, of begging the question, and something very close to outright medical fraud, hence assault of the patient.

When it comes to wireless radiation not only non-thermal but also long-term effects are passed over. Selective inaction on evidence appears to be the deception of choice in both fields.

We must expect to be deluged in public relations from the business camp, in an event akin to a military operation. We will also witness the appearance of those disgraceful puppets, the 'mercenary scientist' and the lobbyist. In order to delay protective legislation, only uncertainty need be created.

The dark arts practised in achieving this are considered in David Michaels' *Doubt is Their Product* (2008). A business model that operates at the expense of an essential well-being – consciously, and possibly with the collusion of the State – meets my definition of evil.

The game is given away – by another part of the corporate sector: 'The Electromagnetic Fields Exclusion (Exclusion 32) is a General Insurance Exclusion and is applied across the market as standard. The purpose of the exclusion is to exclude cover for illnesses caused by continuous long-term non-ionizing radiation exposure, i.e. through mobile phone usage.' UK agent for Lloyd's of London, 18 February 2015.

Follow the money.

To emphasise. Governments betray public health and sacrifice groups and individuals for tax yield and for military and commercial advantage, in a type of corrupted collectivism. They were already the biggest liars going.

In getting a public message across, chicanery is endemic. Hannah Arendt looked at the setting down of a version of things to serve particular power interests. The extreme is a 'substitute reality'. Also, any truth can always be rendered as 'opinion', thus downgrading its force in debate.

To these add another ruse, that of the *ad hominem* argument, which is the attacking of your opponent's character instead of addressing his or her evidence. Add a dash of sleaze, or impugn the person's mental health – those old ones.

*

And where are the 'Greens' in what should be the widest discussion? Many appear to have a blind spot when it comes to this technology. For their information: 'By 2015, the wireless cloud had generated up to 30 megatonnes of CO2, compared to 6 megatonnes in 2012 – the equivalent of having 4.9 million new cars on the road.' (Reported in *World Health*

Organization: Setting the standard for a wireless world of harm.
A call for action and accountability by Olga Sheean.)

The technology has been demonstrated to impact, directly and negatively, other life. Plants, birds, bees, for instance. Where are we going to be minus pollinators? Or plus major habitat loss and dead-zones? Yet, generally, we have not shown that we care any which way, preferring to ride with the lies and to gape at the wrecking ball.

*

Yet, for me, for all that has been said, this is about more than the money. I am naturally cautious in my claims but, unhappily, I have been unable to come to any other conclusion than that there is a war, no less, taking place against life itself, against the Creation. The aims are to derail and sully. The many negative impacts of microwave frequencies on living things, including ourselves, are well-known in certain quarters (there is undoubtedly an established military expertise). Weaponisation of the spectrum was not not going to take place, and Electronic Warfare (EW) and RF Directed Energy Weapons (RF DEW) are capable of delivering crowd control, sickness, behaviour inducement, etc., as well as disruption of electronics. The rebel angels, we are told, fell to earth after being cast out of Heaven. Make of that what you will.

*

The proper function of the State is to have the management of emergencies, and the provision of defence, as priorities. My own view on military expenditure is that, in the final analysis, we really cannot have anything to do with a so-called nuclear deterrent. You have to be prepared to use it and this is still an offensive weapon. Selecting the nuclear option would be planet-trashing – an act not dissimilar to a toddler's tantrum. In its indiscrimination it causes the ultimate collateral damage. It is for upstarts, spiritually speaking, although I realise that this is not the language of international diplomacy. Nevertheless, an automatic loss of substance is induced in human beings who join this violence. (Self-harm of the spirit needs to attract a lot more attention.) It is difficult to discount the view that humans, as a whole, are still at the developmental level of the adolescent, and that is flattering us.

Then what if the 'enemy' is not a State, but a transnational grouping? We are obliged to look for smarter, preventive solutions – ones that fall within the true meaning of 'defence'.

Government is to embody the public will too, of course, but it may be necessary to have a Constitution and/or Bill of Rights to safeguard against the executive acting ultra vires or any tyranny of the majority. Removal of narcissistic rancour between sub-groups must be worked for. A constant is to keep one eye on what lies beyond our immediate, self-important concerns, on what is offering itself as next. Mathew 19:29–30 finds Jesus at some of his most uncompromising:

'And every one that hath forsaken houses, or brethren, or sisters, or father, or mother, or wife, or children, or lands, for my name's sake, shall receive an hundredfold, and shall inherit everlasting life.

'But many *that are* first shall be last; and the last *shall be first.'*

To be taken in the right spirit, but it still revolutionises everything. It is our embrace of all beings, never to be withdrawn. We are not used to truth of this intensity. What would the configuration of the economy then be?

Back in the present world, governing authority is also to act as both facilitator and honest arbiter. From the economic perspective there is the matter of crisis in capitalism to be handled. An economy can become like a heart in fibrillation. Preparing for war is a great way to get the former moving again – similar in principle to the treatment of the latter.

Industry is able to provide both the destruction and the reconstruction (!).

In a mixed economy government is the provider of public goods, financed, to the greater extent, through taxation. In the economic design I advocate taxes have a twofold function. First, taxation is a method of (agreed) sharing. Second, the placing of taxes is part of a regulatory process supporting a more felicitous economy. Taxation is already a tool either to keep a lid on inflation or to provide fiscal stimulus.

A fitting example of the second would be in addressing the matter of second 'homes'. This is an uncomfortable occurrence, when so many cannot afford even the rent on a first one. Disparity in the distribution of necessities is not acceptable. So chocolate-box villages, their signals of former poverty ironically now chic, become ghost settlements, especially in the winter. Very few lights visible, with one or two old locals clinging on. The young, financially forced out, go to the nearby towns, maybe; where else is there? Shop, pub and school close, and there is no longer a viable community. The new owners appear to be oblivious to the issues and to the resentment generated around them.

When whole areas are affected you had, for instance, the Highland clearances in Scotland, where people were removed for more profitable sheep-farming. No-one wants to live in a museum, but this is one of the nastiest things going – the extinguishment of a culture. The loss of a language itself takes from the world a way of seeing, and a tradition of being informed by the spirit of the land.

My remedy is to triple, as a first step, the Council Tax on these properties – no discounts – in order to raise funds to build local, affordable housing. Simultaneously this accommodation would be architecturally in keeping with the genius loci. The levy will, in time, be adjusted to reflect fully the 'externalities' of the purchase of this luxury and to take account of gain on investment. The policy need not be out of balance with a tourism industry. Raising the LTT (Land Transaction Tax) surcharge can help deter this kind of entry to the market in the first place, as will demanding a minimum annual letting duration to deal with the middle-class fraud of claiming your place to be a business. In addition there are planning regulations to be tweaked.

*

Furthermore, good governance has corporate law that is up to date and fit for purpose. Not the type actually written by corporations themselves, which is then rubber-stamped as statute.

When companies are global surely they are liable for a tax that reflects the quantity and profile of their trade in an individual country – if equity and national sovereignty are held to be important. Political will can simply negate the accounting stratagems of private companies, and brush aside all their legal artifice. Any bluffs are to be called – there will always be those willing to trade and cut a deal. This is a strength of the market.

At the company level there is the tendency towards oligopoly / monopoly over the long period. This requires a degree of oversight in order to protect both consumers and suppliers from the potential for exploitation.

Within the trading cycle (a given, as are exogenous shocks to the economy) the State is in the position to provide direct support together with socially and environmentally useful projects at times of high unemployment. These last can build necessary infrastructure, arrest decline in the environment, and need not clash overly with a future economic upturn. This policy is now no doubt mocked as being completely old-fashioned, but just crunch the numbers. Importantly, people remain valued, and great resources, including time, are not wasted. I remember the Thatcher administration, through slavish devotion to an economic dogma, squandering money from the North Sea oil bonanza – a one-off – on unemployment benefit for millions rather than investing in widely beneficial work and forward-looking projects (a sovereign wealth fund included). It also gave us the shift in tax burden from direct (income) to indirect (expenditure), unconvincingly in the name of choice. This hits the less well-off. Now 20 per cent goes in VAT. We live still with the legacy of Margaret There-is-no-such-thing-as-society Thatcher and her 'Nasty Party'.

It is right for people to contribute if they can. 'All that matters is love and work' (attributed to Freud). Earnings from employment enable a person to release a talent or follow a vocation, as well as making service possible. What is not right is to bully benefit claimants into a search for jobs that are simply not there. This has more than a whiff of ritual humiliation about it, and looks to me like victim-blaming in operation. It is reinforced by the use of value-laden rather than descriptive terms, such as 'benefits' over, say, 'democratically-approved social insurance entitlements'. And it ending at the food bank? That these places exist is testament to the public's generosity. That they have to exist disgraces the State and, in time, us.

Neither must there be the attempt here to press individuals into a handful of bureaucratic categories for convenient assessment. People's circumstances are varied and intricate, and refined judgements need to be made in each case. These are probably the most economic decisions in the long run, anyway. The outlay for such a system may be slightly higher, but is justified both financially and ethically. Fairness keeps the short- and the long-term in equilibrium.

Another false economy is a health care system that does no more than patch people up for sending back to the coal face. A broad alternative is to countenance illness as transformational crisis. This is to work with the symbology of symptoms whilst seeing the person as both an inherently homeostatic and becoming entity.

Yet it must go both ways. A publicly funded health service is another part of the welfare economy. People have responsibilities not only to themselves but to the wider community, and it can be argued that those who have knowingly abused or risked their health make, where practicable, a supplementary contribution to any treatment. The judgement, however, is susceptible to doubtful and cherry-picked data, and to a prejudice that can explode into histrionic moral outrage. Alternatively, society may vote for limits on censure through a 'no-fault' health provision paid for out of general taxation. Revenue may already have been raised by high levies placed on certain goods to discourage consumption. The tax on a packet of fags is fierce.

Nor must anyone be abandoned. There is a regrettable tendency in our times for the unfortunate to be viewed with great impatience or even contempt. Perhaps this is a consequence of the complement of fear being hatred. When winning is so trumpeted, 'loser' becomes a term of abuse.

If automation accelerates and takes care of more of the work, then I cannot accept that there will no longer be significant occupations for the majority. We decide. The question will be about how a spectrum of purposeful living is to be catered for, given this development. Besides, is artificial intelligence the subject of an ecstatic hype? Remember recent history. The claim that nuclear power would be 'too cheap to meter' comes to mind. But I do expect humans to be deemed too dangerous to get behind the wheel when driverless vehicles become established. And it is not going to end there. Risk-taking behaviour is part of what it means to be human, but the coming new world will not be brave.

Sheer pace of change, however, may leave predictions looking quickly quaint. But it is fitting to hold in the mind images of a human being hunted by a pack of armed drones, or of your door broken in by a seek-and-destroy robot.

Life is not the machine; it is of the Source, not fabricated by humans.

*

Then there is the matter of the money supply, no less. It is reasonable to expect some democratic overview here. Thomas Jefferson gave the warning: 'I sincerely believe that banking institutions are more dangerous than standing armies. If the American people ever allow private banks to control the issue of their money, first by inflation and then by deflation, the banks and corporations that will grow up around the banks will deprive the people of their property until one day their children will wake up homeless on the continent their fathers conquered.'

The alternative is a central bank providing the nation's currency – as much as is needed to run the economy with stability. Commercial interests are thereby cut out, and independence for this bank prevents the government from playing around with the money supply for its own advantage, when it is politically expedient to do so.

Global financial flows invite regulation within desired limits; homeorhesis is usually preferable. The integrity of the organism is thus maintained.

*

Another service that has largely been taken over by the State is the provision of formal education. The character of this has an obvious connection to the economy – an investment in human capital. *Educare* – to bring forth. Wouldn't it be great to elicit everyone's talents? This could be at once a respect for God's gifts and the foundation for a creative, confident and able people. And not forgetting 'The kingdom of God' that is within us – Luke 17:21. Which is a problem for the status quo.

To quote Churchill: 'Schools have not necessarily much to do with education... they are mainly institutions of control, where basic habits must be inculcated in the young. Education is quite different and has little place in school.' The uniform is a giveaway. Think also of the symbolism of the tie; the very word tells you what you need to know.

Therefore there is the most serious conflict of interest at the heart of public 'education'.

The individual, within this regimen, is to become part of a great construct. Aspiring to anything other in life is not necessary. It is a Dickensian picture of having no ideas above your station. Subordination is fostered by indoctrination, and those so processed are, as a result, kept down through their own programmed 'consent'. Policing of oneself complements that coming from the cops and the courts.

Actually, it is through authenticity that a person is impressive. Imagine the magnificence and gravitas at the dawn of the world. By contrast, those reading from a prepared script, no matter how well this is done, remain flimsy things.

Take a look at some of the faces of the young people as they leave their schools on a weekday afternoon. The eyes, expressions, pallor perhaps, are telling. As are the volume of the voices, characteristic gait and other body language. It has been a factory shift.

For human *qua* person though, the liberation to be derived from a rounded education is great. From a Marxist standpoint, Antonio Gramsci's view, as I understand it, envisioned intellectuals not being an aloof élite, but instead operating in every social stratum. Their presence in the working-class was needed to deal with the forces coming at it from the Establishment.

Likewise there is this from John Philpot Curran: 'The condition upon which God hath given liberty to man is eternal vigilance; which condition if he break, servitude is at once the consequence of his crime, and the punishment of his guilt.'

For the commonweal, real education – the most personally involving possible for each – is paramount. Not pap, not half-truths, not training masquerading as educating. Not time being filled up. No rambling and irrelevant syllabuses. No books that make one temporarily stupid after having read them.

No wonder it is simply not cool to be some kind of swot, or someone jumping through the hoops, if this kind of thing is being foisted upon you.

Unfortunately, I still see no momentum for change, despite there having been so much radical (and quality) thinking done on the subject, along with there being continued unrest. Teachers may jeopardise job and career if they openly challenge the system, and the parents are complicit too, I am afraid. Is the truth just too irksome – or painful – for many of them to look at? The gloomy monolith remains.

I remember the vast amount of my time taken up by school. Blown, most of it – in an open prison. It could have been an educational adventure and an encouragement for learning throughout life. Some hard graft will always be necessary, but looking back, how much better to have been introduced to, say, making furniture, playing the harpsichord, and street-fighting (as awareness for self-defence). How about an option to choose dance instead of games? I do not wish to whinge. Perhaps there was, after all, some valuable self-knowledge to be gained from a cross-country run in the horizontal rain. Maybe you can sign on for the climbing wall these days. The point is appropriate challenge.

If schools have to exist, I offer some suggestions. The first is for special emphasis to be placed on learning to think *and* debate. People will then have a lifelong confidence to speak out on subjects that concern them. Genuine expertise will, and should, continue to be consulted, but the cult of the expert – an effective piece in the repertory of domination – need not be bought into. Awareness is to be established, with the 'curriculum' determined by how the individual responds to various material. Information, of whatever quality, is to be used to frame onward questions; it is never to be taken undigested.

The second for all violence, however it presents, to be transformed into peaceful resolution. Given a flexible curriculum, perfectly possible in most cases. The institutional ethos has to be an unflagging respect for what being human entails. No more control through mortification. Then there is a chance for destructive values and behaviours to die out with the generations. This should not be seen as social engineering.

Third, and most basic, for the five senses to be cultivated to haiku sensibility. As expressed by Zen author D. T. Suzuki, 'to live in the world as if walking in the Garden of Eden'. This prepares comprehension, and complements analysis. Philosophically phenomena need to be perceived for their existence to be complete, for them to come forth from reality's substratum. A thoroughness can then begin to soak in, enabling the creative mind to make new connections spontaneously. To be alert, fully, is to provide oneself with a sufficiency. Yet note that the mind where it meets the world is like a dog returning the thrown stick to your feet, craving that you throw it again.

Fourth, and arguably most important of all, for play, in its broadest definition, to be at the centre of educational philosophy. To develop applied intelligence. Remember that children soon drop the toys that are substitutes for childminders, and would be off roaming, trying out new things. This kind of play creates engagement, expression and self-reliance. Then difference can be 'normal'.

Fifth, in rounding off, for the accent of educational material to be on partnership, not a rule over, and on replacing judgementalism with judgement. Also for there to be an engagement with emotional literacy, to have beauty admitted to the idea of truth, and to understand that recurring stories supply our values. There is a conversation to be started up in the background with the Universal Mind, too.

Changes such as these may have to occur before other, long-hoped-for, system-wide ones can emerge. Similar to learning to walk before attempting to run. There is the old joke of a traveller walking down the road: upon encountering someone coming the other way, and asking for directions, he receives the reply of 'I wouldn't start from here.'

Note, though, that venerating only knowledge will produce another Fall for humankind.

*

Tertiary education allows more personal choice, but I assume that a business orientation has been strengthened by the introduction of student loans. For the student, a return on the investment is required to pay back that loan. As with mortgages, one is pressed towards political conservatism. The existing economic order continues. The knowledge gained at these establishments, especially where future professional application is concerned, must come with a strong sense of its own limitations. My suggestion for a university motto is taken from Molière's *Les Femmes savantes*: 'A knowledgeable fool is a greater fool than an ignorant fool.'

The intellect tends to confuse thought with objectivity. It can only look from the outside, but never knows its actual co-ordinates. It becomes addicted to its own creations, which include more towers of Babel. One does not wish to see it, as in the Peter Principle in management, promoted to the level of its own incompetence.

*

Thought-direction is virtually cemented into place by broadcasting, and by the media as a whole. I hold this entity to be at least as dangerous as private organisations controlling the money supply, or generals being able to cancel the result of an election. Mark that, in Britain, the security services have a long-standing relationship with the legacy media, and oversee its output. Naturally, having power over the dissemination of information, and what slant it is given, is to possess a fearsome influence over others' decisions. Things are bad when television – or the screen – has become the chief reality, defeating all rival versions.

Yet base appetites and the supposed demand for entertainment are happily indulged. Gratification is encouraged. It is not my intention to sneer, but the last Saturday evening (family?) TV show I watched was really rather shrill and desperate, which overshadowed any 'fun'. I suppose it could have been more dispiriting. Popular culture was disdained by Critical Theorist Theodor Adorno as a distraction that keeps the populace unaware of its true state. There is also a sinister potential for an authority-sanctioned personality to be carefully crafted and promoted across the spectrum of programmes, especially in 'soaps', where a favourite character or two can pooh-pooh targeted opinions. This is social engineering, which is not anybody's job. Then there is the claim that people can be acclimatised to the coming new normality, however abnormal that turns out to be. Simultaneously, the punters are to be kept afraid. A lot can be done with (or should that be 'to'?) a demoralised populace. Not much pressure for truth will come from this quarter. Morality and morale are linked.

If only piecemeal change in this industry is possible then a sizeable public service obligation, with guaranteed independence, is to be included as a condition of the granting of licences. One hopes this would support a necessary rationality, and so guard against various madnesses taking over. Note that the main stream has a record of fomenting public outrage. A type of 'infotainment', yes, but indignation can fall in neatly behind predetermined or preferred State policies, especially when it comes to choosing war. Rabble-rousing is an important lever, and the plebs get to feel involved. The notorious 'they' exploits power imbalance, and the mass of the media is necessarily, wittingly or no, integral to its provocation or 'false flag' operations.

*

One could attempt to opt out of conventional society by adopting an alternative lifestyle. Individually, by example, or communally, in dedicated groups. However, there can really only be a partial separation from the whole. Mass action should not be relinquished as this is probably going to be the only route to decisive change. Shelley again:

'Rise like lions after slumber
In unvanquishable number –
Shake your chains to earth like dew
Which in sleep had fallen on you –
Ye are many – they are few.'

In Shelley's time there was the appropriation of the common land through a programme of enclosure. Hence any meaningful self-sufficiency was eliminated for most countryside dwellers, transforming them into a rural proletariat. Their poverty would supply the manufacturing towns with labour. Britain became the first out-and-out industrial nation, but at grievous human and cultural cost. The upper stratum survived the political turbulence.

Nevertheless it does follow, in the words of Thomas Paine, that: 'Every proprietor... of cultivated lands, owes to the community a ground-rent... for the land which he holds.'

At least.

*

Sense of entitlement is a hindrance. Indeed, if you have a bad dose of it you are already halfway to becoming a criminal. Many, in their lives, tip over into arrogance and rapacity, but to be born into a milieu where these qualities are promoted and *de rigueur* is ill-omened. Most of us would get moulded, with no return.

Steps towards a guided enterprise economy, where sustainability is given its due place, can be taken starting any time. Quotas, which fix the magnitude of demand to be satisfied or the scale of human impact, internationally agreed and maybe tradeable, are one option – but the devil will be in the detail.

Shock is another, to be considered when faced with existing attitudes. There is much that is shocking about our present state, if we were not looking so hard the other way. However, I would always want the energy of positive choice with us. The negative is only a return to zero. A call for some element of theocracy – effectively rule by clerics deputising for 'God' – is likely to come from some quarters. For me, though, this carries with it too many dogmatic dangers; if attached more to the letter than the spirit, rigidity is a real risk. The spiritual is often carried by paradox anyway. Also, I cannot see it sitting happily with the Western liberal and Enlightenment traditions. Nevertheless, this voice must be given a hearing, not least for the avoidance of prejudgements. Wherever wisdom comes from is welcome.

The case for judicious economic values, which are actually on the side of life, has always to be made, and the numbers shown to add up. I think it was George Monbiot's point that (paraphrasing) to focus on growth means that inequality does not have to be addressed. There must be an alternative to Galbraith's 'Private affluence and public squalor'. Ideally, a critical mass of support would be reached. However, this is going to be a process, one already outlined by the great Schopenhauer: 'All truth passes through three stages. First, it is ridiculed. Second, it is violently opposed. Third, it is accepted as being self-evident.'

Consequently, I would not exclude, in principle, direct action, as long as it did not take us, as beings, to a lower level.

The best overall stance is presented by Martin Luther King when he talks of 'meeting physical force with soul force', and of refusing to hate.

*

The psychologist Carl Rogers saw the core of people as good. I hold this as both true and propitious, inasmuch as policies based on this axiom make use of the power of self-fulfilling prophecy. I know we are a difficult bunch, but it is too easy to write off humanity, and to slight how dazzling we can be.

Remember that for everyday life to be possible the placing of trust is unavoidable. In any case, there is enough of a recourse available should things go wrong. Traditionally massively so, with punishment (in itself a suspicious notion) often being out of proportion to the 'crime'. This is the only approach the old mind seems to comprehend. Balances, as ever, have to be struck. Instead of having all the baggage that goes with 'punishment', I would replace the word with 'consequences' – outcomes that are understood from the beginning and that are geared to positives. Difference in emphasis is all, and responsibility remains for both sides. In the Christianity I know, I have always been impressed by the promise that there is always a way back.

It has been my experience that most people want to do some good. There is a sense of completion in this, even an experience of 'coming home'. However, they need opportunity, and not to be always under so much pressure, like a delivery driver delayed by unexpected road conditions (there is a job that needs re-designing). Then the 'noble aspiration' of Ortega y Gasset can live, and Ruskin's words will register: 'There is no wealth but life. Life, including all its powers of love, of joy, and of admiration. That country is the richest which nourishes the greatest number of noble and happy human beings.'

Culture And Values

Chains of the past

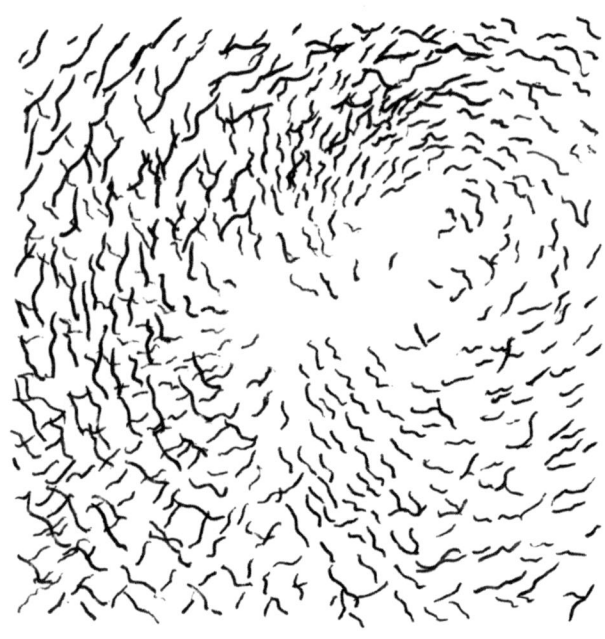

Telling ourselves that some new technology, so far unknown, will save us from our depredations of the natural world will not do. There is abdication on our part when we need to be rescued from the consequences of our own behaviour. Technical fixes though, it appears, will always be preferred to moral examination. We are in a sorry state when an unending self-justification combines with the relentlessness of multiple means.

As for any future advanced applied science, one wonders how much of it is stored up already in the form of patents, waiting to be released by private interests, whose concern will be a maximal income stream over time. Or by the security arm of the State, in projects placed under layers of secrecy. The 'Great Game', that rivalry between nations, is still being played. Its tricks can get very dirty, with expense of human life being largely irrelevant. Even the legitimate concern for defence can become so heightened that it begins to turn into aggression. Whether there is another game going on behind this one is another question.

A clear conception of what we can know ourselves to be – to follow thinker Frantz Fanon – will be necessary in moving to a new economic modus operandi. To assert oneself as a sovereign being, inhabiting the 'common treasury' that is the earth, is a good place from which to start. Then to realise that each is a connected part of all that is, with humans being endowed with self-consciousness and something that it is practical to assume is a limited free-will. It is a spectacular universe, possibly highly improbable (if this is a meaningful thing to say), and unjust restraint of one person by another simply need not be accepted.

My leaning is towards an ethos of constructive competition within a commonwealth. I understand the original meaning of competition was 'to strive together'. Within such an arrangement, there is a greater chance for individuals to find their niche. The best prospects for success are indeed in a team of all the talents; evolution equipped the tribe to be set up in this way. Natural self-development is to be encouraged – it will not need too much ego energy. It is also not ego if one has dedicated personal accomplishments to something greater.

Service is already lauded socially, and an honours system reinforces it. Many other awards are waiting to be given out too. This is almost an industry in itself, although one has to question the reasons behind many of the accolades.

The ideal is where the act is its own reward, but conferring distinction, publicly, does validate, and helps set a tone. And we all like to be stroked a little, so to speak. Still, I can think of no greater tribute than simply to be thought of as a good guy, a mensch.

All this is in contrast to those things we term winning and losing. Alfie Kohn, in his book *No Contest*, argues convincingly that competition does not allow quality to emerge, but instead undermines self-esteem and embitters relationships. Kipling famously called triumph and disaster 'those two imposters'. Unfortunately, the media has been, all along, telling you just how inadequate you are in every respect.

The choice of competing leads naturally to sport, a major preoccupation in our civilisation. Given its position, periodic public examination is warranted. Is it really a war substitute? Gamesmanship easily turns to cheating, then it is fisticuffs. I suspect that, at the very least, it developed as a preparation for conflict. And, most definitely, it is loaded with symbolic meaning, even being part-ritual.

Bringing the mind off-piste for a while, I liken going over for a try in rugby to success in fighting your way into the foe's settlement, and playing the ball in cricket to punching your adversaries and putting them on the floor. Football is worse – scoring is a killing. Its ball crossing the line into the goal is death, and it bulging the back of the net the triumphant display of the corpse. While we're at it, a trophy is the severed head of the enemy chieftain, and a medal the choicest plunder. Do not abandon yourself to sport, and stop thinking its results matter. Move from contesting to improving something. The ability to perform in a grim confrontation, passed down by the ancestors, is kept, and should remain, in reserve.

It is back to the literal in the blood sports (double euphemism 'field sports') which, after inspection, do not really qualify as sport at all. Today they amount to an impudent, but puny, assertion over nature, and a fun day organised around slaughter.

Sport implies equal challenge to the participants. To turn fox-hunting, for example, into a proper one, my modest proposal is the following. If, after a given period, none of these creatures has been caught (and inevitably destroyed) by the hunt, one member of its party, chosen by lot, is to be torn to pieces by the hunters' own hounds, like Actaeon in the myth. If one chooses to play these deadly games, at least make them credible.

We'll stop there. I have no longing to return to the Roman colloseum. I wish us to stir from our – to use philosopher Immanuel Kant's phrase – 'dogmatic slumber', and for us to leave enveloping darkness and the played-out worlds of the past.

Actually, it is reasonable to judge sport not to be creative or constituting recreational play at all. Rather it is another form of work, socialising us for a life where everything is strife. It is more divide-and-rule, and entrenches the existing outlook. Hence it is politically useful, including being a mass diversion. Part of the attraction of a game is that it is important and not important at the same time.

I wonder why we continue to place ourselves in yet another realm of abstraction, instead of operating squarely in a life that is the most present possible. I do accept that taking sides in sport may be ceremony, an identification with the group within which one has one's existence. There is also the wish to emulate the Creator Gods in fashioning these worlds, seen too in the attraction to bringing into being a race of machine servants. Nevertheless, together with the vicarious demand of the spectators, organised sport is tantamount to madness, albeit a socially-approved kind. It creates spurious separation, and corrodes standards of courtesy. The fate of the participants is found in Matthew 26:52: 'All they that take the sword shall perish with the sword.'

I remember one summer here friends and I coming across, on the beach, a sandcastle competition. Announced by loudspeaker, it followed a sadly somewhat frantic kids' kayak race. Filling up the children's time seemingly innocuously, I know, but the format was surely inappropriate. Taking a closer look, who were the judges anyway, and what was their fitness to judge? (Let's get serious here!) How many times do children need to be told that if they do not *win* they are nowhere? How many times before they are subdued for life? Better for the judging to point out what was good about each effort – as celebration. Then quirky talent, unexpected solutions and diversity would not be discarded; nor would the fellowship and mutual respect that could have been generated in the situation.

'Blessed are the peacemakers: for they shall be called the children of God' (Matthew 5:9).

But what we witnessed was the enthralment of the British middle classes – the officer class of the system – to worldly place and position.

Co-operative games, not necessarily any less challenging, are an intelligent alternative. Furthermore, they are potentially a lot more fun. I like the idea of another Scrabble®, where players attempt the highest combined total. It is 'win-win', as opposed to 'win-lose', and a goal is still there to be achieved. Given pooled information and an absence of spoiling moves, I expect the combined score of partners could be significantly in excess of the sum of the individual tallies of opponents.

Related in principle, I gather that the cross-cultural studies of Margaret Mead led her to the conclusion that, when considering maximising production, cooperation is more effective than competition.

So competitive sports should be approached very carefully indeed. The trickery employed in some, moreover, borders on a very public self-abasement. Victory celebrations of players have become roaring and outlandish, faces twisted into the unrecognisable. The triumph appears to be more about relief than happiness. To what extent do these behaviours come from the economic atmosphere of the time? Maybe I could live in a world where there are still gurning competitions, though; the philosopher has an eye for absurdity. An observation from the Sufi tradition is apposite: in alchemy, the turning of lead into gold is a remarkable matter, but more remarkable still is when man turns the gold of himself into lead.

The very design of a stadium, with its 360 degrees of focus, abets exaggerated importance and cruelty of spectacle. Capacity may be maximised, but I have to argue for their redesign as forms that do not pump up the performance so, like a muscle-man's torso is. In my world, architecture – the building's gesture, the style of its spaces, texture of materials – should, broadly, have an elevating effect on human beings. What, indeed, is the relationship between architecture – the reification of number – and people's thought-worlds?

Crude and obvious playing the audience, no. I'd never have made it in showbiz.

The rules of a game, a parallel of ways of doing things in other spheres, should not be exempt from a second look. To decide on one's own set need not be petulance, but instead could be a way of enhancing possibilities. In my family, Scrabble® has become a type of jazz. 'Cheating' is not necessarily banned, provided it is interesting and adds to the event. Joining us in a game could be a different experience!

*

My ideal for a functioning collective places a strong emphasis on a deeper harmony, one that is dynamic, not something that barely joins up the dots. In music, I am often taken by surprise – astonished even – by the harmony. So powering and right, it speaks to the innate optimism of life itself. So much more than the sum of its constituents, it bestows a luminous aura on the sound. Bach's 'Concerto for Two Violins in D minor', BWV 1043, where the two parts move around one another, diverging and converging, then intertwining, is a great piece to experience, even internalise. It would be a good selection to have played to people held in a long telephone queue! If you do not know this composition, its second movement, truly, is the gaze of an angel.

There must be so many pieces where this concord is pre-eminent, rather than, say, melody or rhythm. I am thinking of Pachelbel's 'Canon in D major', which, curiously, never seems to become tiresome. Maybe that is because I hear in it a tender saying yes to birth, death and the bit in-between. All of it. Then, more to the extreme, there is Matteo da Perugia's *Le greygnour bien*, from the late fourteenth century avant-garde, a movement set against the background of the popes and anti-popes in Avignon, France. It is an obscure choice, but a distinguished one.

Harmony indicates an underlying ordering of reality; falling away from this inevitably has negative consequences, which could be read as 'punishment'. In fact, wrong actions actually repudiate existence's coherence – through them one bases ones life in contradiction.

*

In all the arts, music's ability to reach and touch us is unsurpassed. If I were a half-capable musician I would want to be in a band performing, on the one hand, music of joy, and on the other, songs of people's stories – songs of empathy and solidarity. Singing proclaims dignity. To tour wherever people would have us; my ministry, if you like. These daydreams apart – sadly that was not me on drums on Stevie Wonder's 'Uptight (Everything's Alright)' – it will be important for artistic integrity to keep the output of the music sector more 'music' than 'product'.

Music induces states of expanded awareness, and makes paradox palpable. A piece by composer Anton Webern is more silent than silence, and a glorious musical display of infinity comes from Bach. I accept that form is limitation, but these are ways in. Singing from the heart also releases a voice, therapeutically intensifying an individual's occupation of space and time. The need for image is lessened – and one may choose to collect fewer objects.

The arts are not little luxuries to be put back into the box. If you have the zest to be open, your world might get changed, possibly comprehensively. You will have been asked to reckon with yourself. 'Art is a lie that makes us realize truth', Picasso.

However, there will always be those who will not, or who are unable to, take their places in a more comfortably-integrated society. Continuing the musical theme, these lines from *The Merchant of Venice* inevitably come up:

'The man that hath no music in himself,
Nor is not moved with concord of sweet sounds,
Is fit for treasons, stratagems, and spoils:
The motions of his spirit are dull as night,
And his affections dark as Erebus:
Let no such man be trusted.'

The sociopaths are a noteworthy category. The condition is investigated by Martha Stout in *The Sociopath Next Door*. Estimated at four per cent of the population, these characters are apparently capable of doing almost anything to get ahead, and are untroubled, unhampered, by conscience. The conjecture is that their function is to do the dirty work for the group. This personality can cause disproportionate harm *within* a group, however, and so must be identified and neutralised. Pretty well most of us will have encountered the trait in daily life, and the experience may have left us feeling perplexed. Removal of source is best, and we may have to be content with these individuals remaining a permanent entropy within the working whole.

Were not our hands full with people's jealousies, plotting, blaming, grandiosity, emotional chill, them not being up to the job, and their speciality, that of taking offence? (Incidentally, if not a consequence of varieties of narcissism, is offence the result of an over-reliance on external validation?) Often friendship, in practice, does not appear to count for very much here. It is thrown away, like some fast-food packaging being bundled out of the window of a moving vehicle. We are odd, flitting animations, both needy and unreliable, taken up by little dramas. I admit to being one of those people who, having bought a lottery ticket, is surprised at not winning. The world is a big therapy group to which its members are not turning up. We were already dealing with the Awkward Squad. Now this lot. Unfortunately so.

There may be spontaneous reaction to sociopathic behaviour (when it can be isolated), but this needs to be followed through with action, not by vague, continued excuses for the perpetrator. It is lamentable that a determined response from the majority is not more in evidence at the political level. When the people are docile they have been accused of constituting the greatest oppressor of all. This is something that Orwell and Robert Tressell (author of *The Ragged Trousered Philanthropists*) would have understood. When sums of money involved are huge we are in more danger. It is now not just a snack to trigger the predator. Those parodic 'James Bond' master-villains are out there, waiting to be.

'Regular' folk are not entirely exempt, and can be entranced by evil. Being creatures of ambition, this is one of our weaknesses. A daring short-cut appears exhilarating and madly sweet.

*

Moving along in the culture, the built environment needs creation with great care, or enlightened adaptation (just as Feng Shui works with what is there). Continuing from above, architecture and planning do impact us in so many ways, subtly altering both our conception of ourselves, and ideas of what is possible. The baptistery in Pisa and Blaenavon Workmen's Hall, for example, are in the category of buildings that inspire more than they show off. You will not be surprised to hear me call for beauty (that is not plagiarised) and a higher order of design, for grace sustains the spirit. Rank ugliness is not acceptable; it is disrespectful of us, and indicates the taking of too much by those responsible for it. In projects one expects consultation with end-users, then there can be a partnership of talent and democracy. Accountants are not to be in charge, please.

Regarding the existing stock we should always inquire about the source of the money that financed it, even, or especially, where the most benign or charitable of schemes are concerned. So, how much of beautiful Georgian Bath – its style so cool and assured – was built with slave profits as a speculative property development? It is not just gross opulence that is stained.

Incidentally, for the sake of all parties, and in any other set of like circumstances, I recommend thought be given to apology and recompense, philosophically and actuarilly fraught though these may be. (Certainly the further back in time we go the more this thinking will lack sense.) As reconciliation, not perpetuation of a dichotomy of aggressor and aggrieved. Is this a feature of the foreign aid programme? A curse (in its widest sense) can then be lifted.

As enslaving, pillage and exploitation have been global historical phenomena, this reckoning will apply everywhere. Grounds could be economic retardation, culture destruction, inherited trauma and residual incivility.

Traditionally attention will have been drawn to structures and settings that stand for power; 'representational', to use the philosopher Jürgen Habermas' term, to the lower order of society (that most feared of groups). It is always illuminating to see to whom statues are erected. Public spaces are important to members of a functioning society. Intended space is as crucial as the silence between musical notes. It is another type of presence. Gatherings, though, have tended to cause authority to become nervous. How much more enlightened to make a genuine attempt to eliminate the underlying reasons for discontent before outbreaks of mob behaviour occur.

Then, at the risk of sounding like one of those blokes you meet in a pub who has an opinion on everything, I am envisaging the land – much of it in valued central positions – that could be released if cemeteries were to be reclaimed, particularly for community use. This programme would have to battle both tradition and superstition, but the truth is that the material world is one of endless recycling, and domain of the 'will to life'.

To digress, how about Life being a *causa sui,* a cause of itself? It does not appear to mind a zero-sum result, where the positives are perfectly cancelled out by the negatives. Moreover, it seems able to generate its own euphoria. It throws parties for no reason. This dynamic can co-exist with a transcendent serenity. Or what if a Creator's nature is to generate that which It is not? Perhaps existence, as commonly recognised, will be revealed to be a game, although I think the Kabbalistic contention that divine boredom lay behind the creation of the world is going a bit far. If game it is, then God, in some sense, is occupying all positions on the field – on both sides. A return to base occurs when time is called or when this separation ceases to work.

All in all, a marked grave sends out the wrong message. I understand the very human yearning to endure on this plane in some way, but the Earth is for the living. For the dead the trip has ended, and they can be honoured, remembered and, most importantly, ushered onwards in other ways.

*

How much will we dare to change? Will our nerve fail? Much of what is familiar, I believe, will remain, as the evolution of mores is historically gradual. Atheism and its promotion will continue to bolster consumerism. There is that car sticker, or whatever it is, telling me that I have one life and that I must live it. The message, actually, is vitiated by being blared, and feels a bit like whistling in the dark. There should be a reincarnationism version.

*

I expect the use of recreational drugs, that practice so hated by the aggressive and regimented State, to continue. I hope, though, with not so much negativity and predation connected to it. Perhaps we humans simply need occasional distancing from reality, along with some taste of bliss. We are spiritual beings indeed. But obviously there is intervention if consumption disrupts the fulfilment of ones obligations or becomes a hazard to others. There is a stronger case for use if it shows other possibilities of how to be in the world, whilst being conscious of the risks of spiritual derailment or disfiguration of the soul. In place of 'drug' more nuanced nomenclature is needed.

It is likely that the taking of mind-altering substances recreationally has, in measure, been permitted as another 'opium of the people'. Is this why the local dealers, who must be known to the police whose patch it is, are not busted, or not often? They would be taken out easily in a sting. Perhaps the authorities are waiting to trap 'Mr Big'. Possibly the gofers are to be kept as intelligence assets, or for a time when favours need to be called in. Part of the picture could always be a shortage of police resources, of course. Or a practical admission of the need to police by consent.

At the macroeconomic level, could the world economy keep going if drugs' revenues were not laundered and re-circulated?

What about other clandestine or stigmatised markets? Prostitution and pornography are cases in point. What do we do about a high demand for something, where attempted suppression might entail highly intrusive policing, for example? Continued purchase and use, furthermore, would bring the law into disrepute, as well as encouraging the emergence of a mafia. The drivers of both demand (biological and civilisational) and supply (economic necessity, coercion and even choice) call for perspicacity and honesty. We are reminded that there is no getting away from the fact that every thought and action goes into determining, collectively, our psychic climate.

Standing back, though, how different are these occupations, essentially, from some work in other industries? Where, likewise, the potential for exploitation is high, the job degrading, and working conditions high-risk. The person is treated as a resource, to be used up if necessary. Something precious is still cast off.

In the case of the sex trade it is not merely an instance of what is meant to be intimate, joyous and fun being commodified, resulting in a diminished remainder. The Goddess is in every woman, the God in every man. Where partners have no regard for each other, the sexual act is really one of joint masturbation. It is also one more example of the objectification of people, an attitude that must be minimised, then transcended, right across the economy. How many would disagree?

An exception is arguably to be found in the historical phenomenon of (sacred) sexual intercourse with temple 'prostitutes', ideally turning one towards venerating sexuality and its place in Life triumphant. Also, in contradistinction to mere promiscuity, 'free love', in my opinion, deserves to be allowed to find its place, instead of being derided as a Sixties' museum-piece. (But nothing creepy!) In truth it comes from a higher plane. The poles of sex are praise and squalor.

Beyond the sexual act lies a beauty that does not have to be possessed. It is both a blessing on the world and a portal.

Much more on this topic is beyond the scope of this short book, and off-the-cuff remarks tend to be more about the person making them than the subject at hand. May I suggest, though, that any moral muddle in legislation over the selling of sex, and related products, is resolved. It does need to be recognised that primal impulses, when combined with imagination and a predilection for play, can produce what to the prissy are shocking results.

Final comment (attributed) on sex goes to Lord Chesterfield (1694–1773): 'The pleasure is momentary, the position ridiculous, and the expense damnable.'

Picking our way through all this is quite a task, one not to be abandoned for a nod and a wink. Nature errs on the side of surfeit in ensuring reproduction. As sexual beings we are agents of this excess. And sex famously sells, in a presentation that can mimic stagy spectacle. A classier example is Krug's champagne bottle. Its shape fuses abstractions of both male and female sexual allure – finessing the obvious popping of the cork. The design, which one assumes to be not entirely subconscious, but will clearly impact on the subconscious, is more playful than vulgar, and done with brio. As alcohol weakens inhibitions it is quite appropriate.

The erotic needs some rehabilitation. It is the other side of the seedy and illicit – transporting and appearing in the clearest hues. Yet it is a force that suggests you turn yourself over to it, which would be a kind of death. It is strange being a human.

*

Another huge industry, though less contentious, is the one supplying and servicing pets. This consumer preference seems such a part of the cultural landscape. Therefore it will be questioned. Our civilisation is founded upon agrarian surpluses from the channelling and manipulation of Nature. Similarly, a pet animal is a package of tamed Nature, as is a garden. Yet the term 'pet' implies an unequal power relationship.

It is not surprising that so many of us keep 'companion animals', given the way humans can treat one another. A pet may be attentive, loyal and utterly charming. It may be alert on different frequencies. Getting one is also a way for the self to manufacture meaning. It is possibly a display of group belonging, too. And many people get lonely, quickly. However, I question whether bringing in a manageable animal can address underlying issues. It may be a disempowering move; at worst it could mean getting stuck in a type of infantilism. The child attaches to the 'transitional object' – teddy, cuddly whatever – in separating from the mother. Is the desire to have a tame animal common to all cultures? I am not sure, but one would not wish these beings to be something of a cross between a prisoner and a toy, no matter how much human affection was lavished upon them. For William Blake:

'A robin red breast in a cage
Puts all Heaven in a rage.'

As little as a silly or thoughtless name conferred on an owned creature is enough to strip it of its dignity. Speying or cutting off the nadgers definitely so. Selective breeding, following some kind of anthropomorphism, does the same.

Worse, though, is exercising absolute rule over another being.

Then, just like horses that are to be ridden, how many of these animals have their wills broken? Sentimentality and brutality being two sides of the same coin? And do not forget all the other – unfavoured – animals that have to die to feed these living consumables.

Still, in contemporary Britain, if you do not coo over a new puppy, or emit other noises of appreciation, you risk social death. Likewise for raising an eyebrow at the product that is ice-cream for dogs.

Is this a civilisation entering stagnation prior to collapse? One coming to the end of its residency?

Before obtaining one of these things and bringing it into a human environment, which raises questions of its own, might consideration be given instead to contributing towards the preservation of habitat for wild and endangered fauna (and flora)? Wildness is a wonder, brimming with being, and totally here and now. Our psyches are restored by being in its presence; you get a hit. At the same time, the planet's heritage, with all the potential, known and unknown, that this has, is protected.

By the way, the Universal Presence is always our companion.

*

In a new economy would we still be able to buy the large single slipper in that tartan (television accessory?), or that giant inflatable hammer (its reason for existing has eluded me), or those cat ears on a band that my daughter had from Claire's Accessories? (Or a flattering mirror?) Part of me hopes so. Frivolity needs to be taken seriously. A whoopee cushion? Well, so long as there was one for everybody. There must be pazazz too. A cappuccino does not work out of a mug, and cake does taste better from a cake fork.

The free market does uphold personal sovereignty. Moreover, quality control is built in; an Economic Darwinism weeds out the weak, pretentious and dictatorial in goods and services. That being said though, the matrix of innovation is development of theory, which has been based in publicly-funded universities and institutes.

The market is not a panacea. There should always be suspicion of 'nothing but-ism' in any guise. In the words of Antonio Porchia: 'If those who owe us nothing gave us nothing, how poor we would be!'

Concluding

Workable progress

Putting spirituality and economics together is like wrestling an octopus. Nevertheless, this should not prevent it (the former only please) being tried. There are a lot of things not being said – continuously. In life all parts of the self desire participation, ideally coming together as an integrated 'I'. Discover your real name. In travelling with the transience one is refined; there is no such thing as failure in the process.

I have not wished to lambast my own country in this piece, however. Criticism can easily turn into a blanket ingratitude. I have been fortunate, and Britain, all things considered, has to be one of the better places in the world in which to live. Equality and justice remain live issues, but we are not plagued by warlords or marauding barons, though I suspect these energies have been sublimated. Opportunity exists for the determined, and there is still a safety-net, albeit frayed, for the unemployed and the sick. The voluntary sector is significant. Some will not find an affinity with the uniformity on offer, but no liberation in this world was ever gained without some barging. Freedom is also inner work and improvising with circumstances.

Still, a louring economic system may cause much of life to become fraught. There is a risk of stasis developing in us as a people, always waiting for something awful to happen.

In Buddhism there is the 'Middle Way', which provides a balance between asceticism and materialism. Correspondingly, as an economic solution, I have advocated a type of mixed economy, one found between communism/socialism and a version of capitalism (the accent being on enterprise). One characterised by personal initiative, and backed by a responsive politics. Nothing too radical to go with so far – the public / private pattern is familiar, probably inevitable.

However, blandly terming it another 'Third Way' I think is misleading. The sheer clout of multinational corporations in the world's economies cannot be overlooked. Ian Fitzgerald, in his book on the Deep State, tells of the Big Tech firms moving substantial assets into offshore bonds, which could conceivably then be unloaded, potentially bringing the financial markets down. Such a category of threat remains an ongoing danger to democracy, although history shows that if you take on the markets you will probably lose. I am also asking for a considerable enhancement of the model in order to counter the dictatorship of simple method. Human idiosyncrasy and unexpected opportunity are not to be crowded out.

Looking ahead I do hope we can release the hold our current idea of time has over us. It makes the mass economy workable – by diktat – I grant, but is still an imposition on reality. The metric system, too, does not reference the natural measures found on the Earth; there is no mutualism here. Ideally an economic activity, at whatever level, occupies its own space, no more and no less, thereby creating its own time.

If asked to have one, the label on my preferred economic model would read something like 'a spiritually-informed regulated-market communitarianism'. A combination of 'bottom-up' and 'top-down' forces, and where psychic income is counted alongside the material variety. If all life and existence is God manifesting and extending, perhaps in cycles akin to breathing, then it is best to treasure the whole – because it is us – over the illusion of (bleak) isolation. Where each person is on the line between 'oneself' and the 'One Self' is the limiting factor. 'Spirituality Economics' is going to be a snappy title but then there should be a 'Spirituality' pretty well everything.

*

People have been saying this kind of thing for ever, but I urge the creation of an environment conducive to the birth – in truth – of an expanded human. To stop travelling around in second gear, if you like. I am going to keep banging on about a new atmosphere and a new zeitgeist, while accepting that, again, these require prior foundations if they are to emerge. This is the matter of this book. From the Christian standpoint the need for God's grace cannot be disregarded, but our own potential is there to be tried. Ability needs only to be matched by a willingness and some oomph. To 'catch fire'. Moreover, as this is about human emancipation, it therefore contains its own momentum, its own teleology. The symbolism of the lotus is apt, with roots in the mud, and the flower resplendent above the water.

Utopian? Not entirely. With real ecological disaster threatened, a shift of this nature is more urgently required than ever. It is most practical to look for change in ourselves, if only to adapt. In Britain, the renowned wartime spirit has already shown that people can step forward (maybe not without a little grumbling) in the face of grave danger. In industrial relations I will always admire the resolve of the miners – and their families – in the great strike of 1984–85. We have been here before.

Second, for a higher public prominence for an independent counsel, one that has earned widespread respect. This to assist in democratic choice, not to replace it. Something in addition to a reactive judiciary and the political appointees to the House of Lords. A return to those other elders? It should have room for the equivalent of an Old Testament prophet. Unfortunately, in spite of it 'owning' a major resource of wisdom, the Established Church rarely speaks out with force on current affairs. It does not appear to be muscling its way to the front to be the people's champion. The temporal and the spiritual are not in equilibrium. In 1 Samuel 8, God warned the people not to have kings, yet it so happens the head of the Church of England is the monarch. This arrangement is hardly favourable to speaking truth to power. You know, all that is required of us is that we stand up for that truth, sometimes at least. In this world, any generosity is the measure of a person, as service is the chief characteristic of an economy that follows the way of the Spirit. The service that is our consummation. To the degree that stumbling human nature can live to this, we (from the Christian point of view) walk with the God who is Love and alongside the Jesus who gave everything.

Then where is the warning about going further down the cul-de-sac of materialism? At least the difference between pleasure and delight could be pointed out. It is a trap to get too comfortable in a fallen state. We can always be renewed by Jesus' radical message; his teachings make it exciting to be a human being. Christianity of whatever variety must be so much more than taking out another insurance policy, so to speak. I have always liked the phrase 'living waters' – The Song of Solomon 4:15.

Having suggested this, though, position and prominence must never trump force of argument or dismiss the testimony of a lived experience. This is only to demand the intellectual equivalent of no-one being above the law. When this goes without saying, the many touted schemes that are really wolves in sheep's clothing are more easily uncovered, and protection is mounted against another dictatorship, the one of the technocratic type. Beware of so-called technical experts given real power. If they are not front men directing more encumberment their mindset will, very probably, oversimplify what it means to be human (necessary to minimise costs in operating a system). Moreover, their pronouncements, in part at least, are likely to stem from whatever ideas happen to be fashionable at the time. We do not have to genuflect before the algorithm either – not any such thing!

All too often I witness argument or report downgraded simply on the basis of the speaker's social standing. On the other hand, those to whom more elevated status has been accorded get away with assertion. Eliminating this kind of nonsense is important for the sovereignty of the electorate.

And third, for disproportionate political power, finally, to be no longer acceptable. Those at the bottom of the heap get zero-tolerance. Let us apply this at the top. It is only a request, really, for people to grow up.

Unrealised potential is thought of as sad in an individual. Why not in a society, or the whole world? Watch out for expecting too little – it's contagious.

However, I do accept that there will be civil disobedience, fraud and all kinds of black markets if the timing of these changes is clumsy, or if the populace feels that things are being imposed on it. This goes for any measure that aspires to regulate the economy; it must undergo its own process of natural selection.

*

I know that campaigning is about values first and probability of success second, but to those who say it is pitiably naïve to trust that a world of calmer satisfaction is possible, my retort is they get away from the jaundiced – or tendentious – depiction of the human being as largely a hopeless animal in need of control, or a mere disturbance in space-time. Alexander Pope again, in *An Essay on Man*, is more balanced:
  'Placed on this isthmus of a middle state,
  A being darkly wise, and rudely great.'
  With the message of the former you get to stay in the 'dark ages', whereas to relish the latter can allow for some first steps in a renaissance. Admittedly it would be better to start with citizens not being undermined by Statist 'education', private interest media 'reality' or a medicine that does not go after the causes of disease, if I may throw all those things in.
  To get there is to travel in awareness – a superior form of travel. There are no guarantees, but higher consciousness offers more options. When you get a glimpse of that living truth (I am thinking of Wilfred Owen's words, 'truths that lie too deep for taint') you believe yourself to be the luckiest person in the world. There is nothing you would exchange for the experience. There will be no looking back.
  Again, there will be many obstacles to surmount, or preferably side-step. Occasional discouragement, as in any endeavour of worth, is to be expected. I see my country vote for more of the same – again. It is in the name, of course; Conservative. To conserve. Fine to retain that which serves, but not the policies that have run out of relevance or even

expose the community to danger. In the Second World War I understand that the Polish cavalry actually broke their lances on the advancing German tanks.

A word on leftist revolution. Philosopher Stephen Hicks, employing concepts from Nietzsche, considers a psychological background; my version is as follows. 'Master morality' is adventurous and purposeful, with life being to its taste. Where a sunny day makes this disposition forget all the terrible yesterdays. 'Slave morality', by contrast, is insipid, timid, restricted. Each outlook would plump for a very different economy. The 'slaves', as well as potentially developing homicidal envy, end up in self-loathing. To cope psychologically they hold up obedience as a virtue while castigating initiative and success, using misrepresentation where necessary. Nihilist resentment is unleashed upon the 'masters', whose confidence and reputation this can undermine. The 'slaves' are too weak to confront them otherwise. Latent conflict is always going to be present in the economy.

In the EU referendum I wondered whether the British were ready to take back greater control over their lives, and reject the non-democracy of the European superstate. The great legerdemain of project Europe was to move from trading bloc to political union without another vote.

Those elected may not like it, but a rolling option for referenda fine-tunes politics, preventing the populace from being bounced into policies they would not choose on a case-by-case basis.

From the economic perspective, a vote for leave must cause concern about access to the single market, and business might consider relocation, or at least develop contingency plans. Financial markets will always factor in uncertainty. The well-known phenomena of consumers postponing larger purchases and companies delaying investment during uncertain times were to be predicted. Vindictiveness (at the level of the school playground) from former political partners, both as a reflex to the 'insult', and to send a signal to other waverers, had to be anticipated too. There are still too many unknowns to make pronouncements, but since there is so much common interest at stake, an inglorious compromise is the likely outcome. Britain can then, if it so wishes, embrace a new role, minus pretensions, with a more arm's-length relationship with Europe – if its own union is able to survive.

Do not be surprised at calls for a 'second referendum'. This trick has been pulled before. The people must vote until the result is the 'right' one. It is a travesty of course, but the masters will be pleased. Equally worrying for expression of the public will is a 'Leave' that is not 'Leave'.

Settling 'Brexit', which recalls Henry VIII's break with the Roman Catholic Church, will take years. Most of the talks at the beginning were about money. It was not edifying. I accept that Britain should honour prior commitments, but beyond these what is the reasoning behind paying to *leave* a club? I thought one paid to *join*. In any case, I am not sure there is any law to support this EU demand.

Also, the European stance on its 'divorce bill' for Britain, in that no talks on trade can take place until some figure is settled upon, is extortion, pure and simple. It is the M.O. of gangsters. A rip-off becomes more understandable with the knowledge that the UK is a significant net contributor to the Union's finances.

Power likes to give itself 'airs and graces'. It even has its own particular smile – one of menace, not the primate signal of peace. All the facial muscles that must go into that! A gang will resort, speedily, to brutal action to protect its interests. Just watch its members move, slickly, between benevolent image and active thug, according to circumstances.

The European Union will keep on rolling. One idea to come out was that of a European army. Another, I believe, was for Europe to have a single president. These should have set the alarm-bells ringing. Study the history of empires. And

I do not think it hysterical to point to the Nazi vision for Europe. I recommend going to see the ballet *Spartacus*. The choreography – another language of course – for the Roman Crassus is an essay in imperiousness, *ex officio*. Pouring off him is casual confidence that opponents will be crushed, which (spoiler alert) is indeed what happens. Times and costumes have changed, but the effect on humans of holding power has not.

Some may say that this sounds like a newspaper editorial written for the consumption of 'Middle England', but I have yet to hear one good argument for a European political union. OK, depending on your views, to offer some protection from a rampant Conservative government at home – but this is our work. Funding for schemes in Britain from the EU? This is for us to do, too. To put it harshly, stop waiting, like a dog, for a morsel to be thrown from the table. It started out as our wealth, after all. The assumption of responsibility is preferable to the uncertainty of dependence. 'A camel is a horse designed by a committee', Sir Alec Issigonis.

Empires, including those in all but name, are doomed given how internal tensions surface with time, and how centralisation is not an efficient way to manage local conditions. An empire is a vain and unstable artifice; originating in more or less violence, it has only a limited lifespan.

I acknowledge the realpolitik argument that a bloc of European nations will be better able to form a balance against powers such as a Russia or a China. However, this can be done by treaty instead of through political (and cultural) homogenisation, taking on board the concept of a group having multiple levels of identity.

I urge the reader to seek out comprehensive and independent analyses of the story. The Brexit majority is likely to have been, in part, a rejection of the surge of globalisation. Emoting about European togetherness is not an argument. I am still finding it strange that nationalist party opinion would have their countries remain in/join the EU after leaving the UK, as this move exchanges one lack of sovereignty for another. Member countries in the east remember their time under the Soviet Union.

*

On that sovereignty: a nation that joins the Euro or equivalent is throwing an important part of it away. Not having a central bank to issue your own currency will, in hard times, threaten a real debt burden or outright insolvency. That State now has to enter the financial markets, very possibly being charged high interest rates on account of raised risk – or go cap in hand for a bail-out, which will almost certainly have an austerity package attached. It is not able to run its own money supply subject to inflation targets – see Postscript.

In leaving this topic it is worth asking whether there is a charge of treason to answer for certain British politicians, officials and (influential) supporters of European integration. Likewise for the monarch who has not protected the Constitution, of course.

Remember that whatever liberty we can muster, even though it will be inadequate, counts for so much. Freedom – to choose – is an indispensable spiritual condition. Here in Wales – historically, politically – there is unfinished business.

*

I would like to say a little about the country in which I live at present. It is a sketchy foray but one that is concerned with how near (or far) practice is to (or from) principles. For me the ways of an economy and related legal measures, if these have not developed historically in situ, are to respect a culture. Theirs is a service function after all.

In the laws of Hywel Dda of 909, where crimes were concerned the remedy focused on restitution instead of

122

requital. This distinction promotes responsibility and inhibits the development of a vicious spiral of revenge. The health of society is prioritised.

The laws also had it that the deceased's estate was to be shared equally among the children – more egalitarian than English primogeniture, although not beneficial for capital accumulation.

The proud radical tradition coming out of the experience of industrialisation should also get a mention.

Any alien overlay on an existing corpus of customs must result in a very deep un-freedom for a people. And group memory is long. How much of the character of our body of law carries over from the rule imposed following the Norman Conquest of 1066? One would suppose conquerors to be big on property rights whilst harsh on even minor infractions of a new legal code. Public execution is a good example of State terrorism. Fear (negative) then replaces sense of proportion (positive) as a guide to conduct within society.

Preventing people from inhabiting their culture disorientates, thus making them easier to boss. They become outlines of persons. The aggressor group might also possess the stupidity of believing it has nothing to learn from another tradition.

To an observer, and not wishing to patronise, it appears that work too is needed on significant words and symbols in circulation in Wales. This is not to be petty, for these glow powerfully in the psyche. A few examples.

First, the actual name of Wales. The Anglo-Saxons called its inhabitants foreigners – Welsh. This term moves from differentiation into discord.

Second, the union flag. It has no Welsh component. It is a reminder of the Anschluss of 1536 (instigated by a Tudor monarch, I grant) and of the attentions of English power before then. The subjected, inevitably, are viewed as second-class citizens, regardless of intrinsic realities or historical happenstance. Jeering is added to fearing the other. The blemish of chauvinism is very difficult to eradicate.

Third, the 'Prince of Wales'. I do not wish to depend on royals (see the warning in 1 Samuel 8), but the title underlines the subordination of Wales to England. (The feathers on the famous red shirt surely have to go.) The last real one, Llywelyn, was killed in 1282.

*

One cannot expect anyone to suck up this kind of thing for ever. At the risk of stating the obvious, a nation's future must balance autonomy – grounded in an authentic and strong identity – with healthy co-operation with neighbours. This is the situation of individual and group. It is also, at the lower level, how the 'building-blocks' of existence itself fit together and function. Then the historical overreach disappears, and life for all is lifted.

Anyone can see that Wales – Cymru – needs restoring. However, unless the policy of the current Welsh Government is one of conscious gradualism, it remains a client administration. On the other hand, people must be wary of a vainglorious independence that relegates bread-and-butter concerns for the pet projects of ideologues who will not be there afterwards to pick up the pieces. Will the administration trade more irreplaceable national heritage and soul-land (and tourism) for big en vogue industrial developments? (Towering wind farms in the Cambrian Mountains where there exist offshore alternatives.) Might it, ironically, dismantle its own civilisational character under the banner of 'progressive' politics, leaving behind only a cartoon identity? The political failure is later to be found on the lucrative lecture tour, in some boardroom or signing copies of a ferociously dull autobiography.

Utopian delusion tends to attach itself to nationalist

movements. Unremittent zeal too. The Law of Unintended Consequences matters little in a 'Brave New World'. Voting for a constitutional separation may lead to even less personal independence under the State – the devil you don't know.

*

Plebiscites apart, one drawback of our system is that short-term policies tend to be adopted to please the electorate, and the hard work put off.

All one can do, in addition to living by example, is to make the points – vigorously and with pride, as I hope I have done in this argument for a happier economy. Universality should be envisioned. Jokes are welcome, too. They have always been the revenge of the down-trodden, and have the knack of bringing matters into a sharp focus. Humour can be a much more effective way of communicating realities, or at least broaching a subject; think of the relationship between jester and king at the mediaeval court. It also stops us bestowing too much reality upon what is impermanent. You may indeed not have won the lottery of life as a pizza delivery driver in Milford Haven with one brake light out, but part of this existence is to be a detached observer of your fate. Derision and empathy lie very close together.

*

What could be some indicators of progress? Well, within individuals there might be a sensation of serenity, or an intuition that one is where one needs to be. There may even be moments of spontaneous exhilaration. And, paraphrasing playwright Bertolt Brecht, when there is thankfulness for one's birth instead of for one's death.

This earthly journey does appear to have struggle (and the rest!) woven into it, contrary to what we are told by those having-it-all 'philosophies'. I am content with notions of doing God's work, or getting back to the Source. Or, from an agnostic or atheistic viewpoint, with an existentialist choice of honourable action, or shining for its own sake. Or again, and mixing Schopenhauer and Nietzsche, partaking of the non-rational and the heroic in a reality that is Will. Dignity is possible even in an absurdist universe, and 'is-ness' provides a ready-made meaning of life. These are all ways to peace, and life will present its compensations along the way.

In coming to the end of this book it is good to remember this from Marx: 'The philosophers have only interpreted the world in various ways; the point is to change it.'

*

There are many recognised national and global measures of betterment, along with conventional ones applying to the individual.

I offer a few – twenty – less routine pointers to what I would define as improvement.

1. Fewer prescriptions for anti-depressants.
2. Fading of the idea of work-life balance; it is all life.
3. Less high-profile charity. Preventing the need for substantial charity comes first. I do not wish to see a beggar class co-dependent with feel-good giving.
4. Fewer betting shops in fewer downbeat areas. When you are desperate the odds for success fade from consideration. And what a winning business formula a lottery is!
5. More of those kit toys being open-ended and genuinely creative, as opposed to the variety that looks like early training for assembly workers.
6. Not leaving industrial scars on the land, or a continent of plastic rubbish in the ocean. To care if there is ugliness.

Nanotechnology fallout will require a higher order of safeguarding.

7. Police not looking like paramilitaries.
8. Celebrity gossip magazines going out of business due to lack of demand.
9. Flags tending not to be brandished so. A nationalism or sectarianism can come about from a past wrong but the country or group so supported may not merit, in respect of its present way of life, such acclaim.
10. Less indulgence in fantasy.
11. When there is more lustre than glitz.
12. Ability to tell when a 'war for freedom' is really a thieving grab for resources.
13. More attempted citizens' arrests on Tony Blair.
14. Not confusing form or image with substance.
15. Ceasing to feed monsters. Not identifying good times with alcohol, for instance. Where one is not self-medicating, drink is fun for about twenty minutes. Then you begin to slow up, and delusion creeps up like a shadow. I want to leave Plato's cave, not go further into it.
16. The fable of the goose that lays the golden eggs being on every Economics curriculum.
17. A worldwide moratorium on commercial fishing coming into being.
18. Fewer of us choosing to dance by ourselves, and even fewer doing so in a premeditated manner – those meaningless automata routines. There is the dance that dances the dancer, bringing in the red of the rainbow.
19. Moving away from colours in clothing that are mean and isolating, and more towards those that exult – and exalt.
20. To act from a dignity – that word again – that resides within (the jewel-presence).

*

One more. Beating off proposals for a cashless economy. It is not necessary to be in possession of an excessively suspicious mind to realise that anyone's access to (electronic) money could be shut off easily, with all that this would entail, or to ask whether any imperious government could resist being able to target people in this way. More subtly, a digital currency that is programmable enables the exclusion, in advance, of certain personal expenditures. This is now not so much money as vouchers for the second class. At the very least the monitoring of your electronic transactions helps construct a profile of you. One then envisages rights becoming granted privileges. No cash = slavery. Maximum deposits, time limits on accounts or negative interest rates swing in to further degrade the financial power, and therefore agency, of the individual.

*

And one more. Recognising that it is desirable for the week to contain a Sabbath. A song requires more than just one note, repeated.

*

I leave with these words from the New Testament. They are emblematic of much of what I have been trying to say:

'Inasmuch as ye have done it unto one of the least of these my brethren, ye have done it unto me.' Matthew 25:40.

'The thief cometh not, but for to steal, and to kill, and to destroy: I am come that they might have life, and that they might have *it* more abundantly.' John 10:10.

Uttered by one Jesus, but the truly spiritual reaches everywhere, unifying, not dividing. Look at what has been on offer all along.

I wish you well.

Afterthoughts

Our best selves

I can see how it might be difficult for an author to finish a book with some satisfaction. Passages already set down inevitably suggest new intellectual or creative avenues. It is like the branching of a tree. What is unsaid can nag, imploring us to give it form and existence. Also, the novel has an unfair advantage over the familiar, in that its allure, the 'glamour', has not yet dissipated. When beholding this season's fashions we reflect on the dull stuff in the drawers back at home.

Nevertheless, tinkering overly with the original piece can lead to it losing both shape and edge. The opus may move towards more of a personal diary of ideas, and away from a pointed presentation. A heartfelt polemic begins to turn into a treatise, sprawling and enervated by qualification. There is nothing wrong with sustained scholarship of course, but my primary intention in writing was to reach an audience as quickly as possible. My brevity is not intended as flippancy.

That being said, I believe it desirable to elaborate on the spiritual and psychological elements of the economic mosaic proposed above, as it is these that will largely determine success or failure. Once again views are personal, even provisional, and suggestive rather than prescriptive. Temperamentally my focus is on the outcome for the whole, wherein sufficiency, stability and justice are satisfied. I take custodianship of the world to be a human service to the Divine Idea, the ne plus ultra.

I will declare economic activity to be for the provision of a sufficient material platform for life, and little more. It is the beginning of an answer to psychoanalyst Erich Fromm's question of 'to have or to be?' He sees the repression of what is best within us on account of it not fitting in with socially accepted norms. To avoid ostracism we go back to calculations and profit and loss, but doing so bypasses the love that actualises us. It is not fitting for the spirit to wallow at a level lower than its own. The economy is to be a good servant, not a bad master, and there to help restore selves crumpled by events. The call is to rise through appetites, out of the machinations of the frightened ego, to the riches of pure being. The 'one pearl of great price' is acquired by selling all that we have. It is to be in the world but not of it, and to cease a life of pipe-dreams and dissolution. This is evolution – a world away from pernicious growth exemplified by a cancer. Bhutan's measure of GNH (Gross National Happiness) is a step in the right direction.

If one is completely present, life is possessed. However, saturation levels of an advertising that is never the 'whole truth' are an alien vibration in the environment, personally invasive and the creator of noise in the mind. This is another form of pollution – more product than bi-product – and repetition is the crudest brainwashing.

Let us have care for our companions on this 'earth walk' too. We need to be reminded that it is easy to find ourselves on the cold outside – through job loss, illness, relationship disintegration, a serious error of judgement, or just fickle fortune. There is that great line from Shakespeare's *Timon of Athens*: 'Men shut their doors against a setting sun.'

*

Hold everything as predisposed to change, responsive to the power of underlying patterns and their fluctuations. One illustration is a cure, the transformation involved in the spontaneous remission of bodily symptoms, another the utter collapse of a tyranny. As individuals we are not to cling to old personae. There are cycles too, and polarity contains the beginning of its opposite. Sandcastles tumble into the returning tide.

I realise, though, that an idea must wait on a person, that its acceptance, or not, is the culmination of a long, individual process. This is why megaphone evangelism is such an unpleasant and inefficient practice. Besides, belief, even if it is reckoned to be desirable, cannot be willed. A great concentration of words, also, easily grows wearisome, which is the drawback of a book! Although these realities need heeding, getting fit, this time intellectually, could be boosted massively by a rethought education service. I have already given schools, as currently constituted, a hard time. They are definitely not about the glory of the mind. If they were, meditation, whose practice, amongst other beneficial things, allows the greater mind, or a state of buoyant awareness, to arise, would have been part of the syllabus long ago. On my long list of reforms for contemporary educational establishments is the one that requests they find a way to contemplate matters we as beings would rather avoid. Through this encounter lies the route to aplomb and resilience.

Still, I well know that humans, myself included, are really very good at providing convincing reasons for not doing particular things, and for not having these confrontations at all. I do not like the harsher meaning of the word, but we are weak, and easily spooked. Panic-buying is a good example in Economics. There is the passage from Matthew 26, where Jesus says to Peter: 'This night, before the cock crow, thou shalt deny me thrice.' Then even Jesus, shortly afterwards, in some of the most moving words I know, pleads: 'If it be possible, let this cup pass from me.'

An active wisdom tradition will help us not keep postponing the vital work. Even if we know we cannot make it alone, we are obliged to become part of the momentum.

Beings who can not only conjure up their own adaptation – from houses to nail-clippers, from terraforming to the hand-held, battery-powered mini-fan – but who also come out with such gestures of High Existentialism as the Charleston and those Biscuits Roses de Reims (pink confections of dubious food value) have something going for them. May the gods be patient.

*

Another of my demands of public education is that it is to operate, consciously and indiscriminately, in developing an awakened and fully responsible citizen, something I realise that has not, basically, happened throughout the whole history of 'civilisation'. To this end I would proffer, at the right time, an Economics primer to students. Just a few economic and philosophical principles are enough to complement common sense. This preparation provides a foundation for oversight throughout the economy. The greater the participation, the greater the protection. There would be an inherent wariness over increasing concentrations of economic power, so assisting in thwarting corporate dictatorship and the authoritarian fancies of the few. One nightmare is a society that is a variant of that depicted in H.G. Wells' *The Time Machine*, with its Eloi and Morlocks. Even short of my economic model, which has its own reconciliation of opposites, wider economic literacy cannot but warn against, for example, another financial crisis, whether permitted or manufactured. There may be insistence that the banking complex is finally nationalised (in a contemporary form) – *pro bono publico*.

Lastly, there needs to be an orientation to making the transition from childhood to (positive) adulthood, rather than just letting bits of ourselves slide into the future in no particular order. The initiation rite could be found in traditional culture. For us today, mentoring, as an option, will help prevent some of the more drastic mistakes of inexperience being made, and encourage a younger another to become their own person, with all the responsibilities that this involves. Keep open, though, a place for play, which enables both hands-on understanding and exploration for better solutions. Relevant for any and every age, it is not fun for no reason. The universe itself may turn out to be pure play, which I suppose is one way of Existence experiencing itself.

*

An economy needs purchasing power to keep it going, which is where a basic income provided by the State for each citizen, mentioned above, could become more prominent. Simultaneously this idea recognises income inequality in society. Is this also a part of how foreign aid might be delivered? In non-emergencies it asserts the individual to be the best judge of his or her own welfare, and would avoid subjecting a different culture to too much of a Western model.

*

A deeper change within us is the one of gathering comprehension, or, in its sudden form, the epiphany. After these become part of us there is no going back to former ways. Subsequent to the most involving of their appearances, a person will simply not, any more, assent to injustice, or participate in the grosser manifestations of socially-accepted brutality and stupidity. In economic choice, consumption is less likely to incorporate compensation for an unfulfilling life, which is akin to comfort eating. That the 'holiday in paradise' is touted at all says much about the state of life for many, real or perceived. The sales pitch is predictable, but the main problems are that you take yourself with you, and that you have to come back. And what is the point of the travelling if you do not have the eyes to see?

Rather, start with the marvels hidden in plain sight. To see all those humble things and recognise that they are perfectly themselves. This is revelation on the cheap.

A desire for kicks at the expense of personal health should fade also. The wasting of time will be seen for what it is, and boredom welcomed as an ally.

*

There are probably many reasons why teenagers hit such an existential crisis, including the biological factors. I believe a significant portion of their anger arises from witnessing adults continually accept the unacceptable. Alongside equating maturity with this hypocrisy, there is typically no reference to the magic that we are here at all. The marvellous has been snuffed out.

Those crappy jobs must have something to do with it, too. Deskilling is increased by the introduction of advanced technology to the workplace. The middle strata of the labour force tend to decline, with the occupation profile returning to one characterised, you might say, by lords and serfs. Young people may find themselves staring at a tortuous semi-life, a future unreasonably foreign. The madness is rounded off when everyone else around you tells you, or behaves as if, there is no other way. Like troops marching off to the trenches, singing.

This being said though, if constructive movement within the psyche can really begin to permeate at the group level, then it will be easier to say no to the crabbed, little life, to the destruction and the world-sorrow. An unpretentious glory waits to be received.

'Man cannot live on the human plane: he must be either above or below it', Eric Gill.

In Christian orthodoxy, moreover, we are redeemed by Christ's sacrifice. Whether a loving – and omniscient – deity requires a blood offering is a fair question, though. Allegory it may be, announcing the need for the restoration of balance after negative human action. Looking at it from a different angle there is the disturbing equation of love with death, as in Wagner's *Tristan und Isolde*. The Christ figure is of the hero archetype, restoring what was lost to the community. Why cannot salvation come through the *life* of a compassionate and enlightened teacher or avatar? We must redeem ourselves – in imitation of Christ, as it were. Atonement is diffuse. The Fall can be put down to a forgetfulness. Jesus had a ministry, after all. 'I am come a light into the world, that whosoever believeth in me should not abide in darkness' (John 12:46). His invitation is 'follow me'. To new life.

This brings us to the camp of the Gnostics, a major alternative to, or complement of, early orthodox Christianity. I would wish to inhabit the spirit of both, with discernment, and gather them up in a creative poise – seeming contradictions notwithstanding. I want the priest, like the doctor, to be no more than a consultant. Exploration is placed above narrative. Again choice must be, wherever possible, for the individual, in an unhurried unfolding.

'Ask, and it shall be given you; seek, and ye shall find; knock, and it shall be opened unto you' (Matthew 7:7).

*

Perhaps I am thinking too literally. Might sacrifice be using the present to build something more effective and durable, something altogether better for the future? It comprises work and delayed gratification, ideas found in both spirituality and economics (saving and investment over consumption). This is not the concept of the scapegoat.

Personally, I am sympathetic to the view of Jesus' final act as being simply one of love and integrity, regardless of consequences. He is on the side of 'the big life'; 'not as I will, but as thou *wilt*' (Matthew 26:39). Jesus' main point is to get to this place, and I would rather the messenger were not placed before the message. My reading is that JC did not come to perform some cosmic ritual but instead to show how to avail oneself of this existence, in a regained freedom. (Buddha likened himself to a finger pointing at the moon.) In itself atonement is at the level of pain, not liberation. Jesus represents the spirit of life, breaking through the limitation that has piled up. There is not a preoccupation with looking back at how one fell short (Aquinas has it that sin is misdirected love anyway). The manner of his death, predictable or not, is then more a worldly consequence of his commitment and actions, and less an intention. The Cross represents love completed. I am torturing standard theology, but his demise (martyrdom) serves to encapsulate his work. We will leave it there.

A teacher is relevant up to the point his or her lessons have been learned. For Father Bede Griffiths, Jesus returns as the Christ consciousness in ourselves, for us to be Love in this world.

My questions are not meant to come with *hauteur*. For those who do not know, there is in Anglicanism a tradition of more freedom of thought and scope for interpretation. Variations on a theme do not make the theme any less important. I have been drawn into doctrine, but welcome comment from both the sage and the seeker.

Yet around all of this remains the danger of getting bogged down in exegesis (and sophistry) for ever. And how we know the terrible history of groups defending their identity beliefs. The cross, actually, is an ancient, world symbol, signifying a realised unity, the quality of being centred, and, in the Latin version, transcendence also. It does provide something of a focus for Jesus, in spite of its heavy quality and a leaning towards the cerebral. It declares, boldly, that the giving of ourselves is the way; this is best understood through experience. However, if the ailing Church were a corporation, the brand consultants would have been brought in.

*

The spiritual life is not just about approving nicely-sliced ideas. In fact these can concrete over the wild of our original nature, leaving us bereft and prone to misery. Like clipping a bird's wings. Reasoning has a calling but also displays an inclination to harass any other mode of thinking – it is in its nature. In John 14:16–17, Jesus talks of the gift of the 'Spirit of truth'. I see in Pentecostalism an openness to the gifts of the Holy Spirit (as termed) – the great transformer. We need some of this, in my opinion, but obviously with the requisite caution. Spiritual sight is to be judged by its fruits. Unless one resonates with a particular version of reality (or ontology), undergoing more than a mind-response, one is only going to be taking on another ideology, and becoming a foot-soldier in someone else's army. This does not meet the required standard of honesty.

Understanding might have to be something like surfing, staying on (with panache) for as long as possible, or a kind of juggling, where all the balls are in the air at once. There also is the human heart warming, registering as something more than an organ that pumps blood around the body. An activated love generates its own knowing, which is more articulate than any idea. Love dwarfs everything else, seen so clearly in Rembrandt's *The Return of the Prodigal Son*. We are already carried by instinct. Recognition succeeds thinking.

I prefer the notion of initiate to that of follower. Obedience is not a final state; following rules is not *it*. A church can get us started but the real work is internal – 'the development of our psychic roots towards the buried center which is the source of Life in us', in the words of Robert Linssen, author of *Living Zen*. Our relationship to that which we call 'God' is not subject-object but how we live *within* that principle. An individual coming into wholeness is going to be less economically chaotic, too.

*

The philosopher Maurice Merleau-Ponty, I think, had the phrase 'seized by life'. I find myself on the side of regarding this existence as more of an amazing privilege, albeit a demanding one. Whichever, we are bound to consider how it is to be treated. In the absence of adequate thought, mystical communion (more or less overwhelming) – or by dismissing, out of hand, a concept like 'Christ in you' (Colossians 1:27) – we are at the mercy of opportunists, tricksters and those who claim to know, and a history of excess and self-important, frequently deadly, fuss will continue.

Instead, if the answers – all of them – are within, as they must be, albeit in intriguing forms, there is the foundation of a self-righting system, everywhere. Its operation will lessen the economic fall-out of *samsāra* and call out misplaced will. It will challenge being led away by comfort (those entanglements of Odysseus with Circe and the Sirens), and us bringing forth an unending series of doomed vanity projects.

'Consider the lilies of the field, how they grow; they toil not, neither do they spin: And yet I say unto you, That even Solomon in all his glory was not arrayed like one of these' (Matthew 6:28).

Postscript

Coronavirus 2020

Pestilence, sadly, is a fixture of human existence. Sometimes the bugs are ahead. On reflection, I am surprised that something like the current affliction has not come along sooner, given globalisation, biowarfare capability and the production of Frankenstein monsters generally. Not only alleged to be the cause of so much direct suffering and death, the virus, wherever it came from, and which still has a way to go, set in motion a slew of indirect effects, including rising death rates from other causes. Whether a 'virus' is cause or effect in the disease process is another discussion. We have had a pummelling, although I wait to see the figures on average mortality and morbidity. Notable, for the subject of this book, has been the parking of the economy. Strange times when the price of oil falls below zero. At least governments, in their intervention packages, recognised that the welfare of each depends on the welfare of all. Let us hope that the coming taxation to pay back the notional debt is structured in the same spirit.

Heading into the future a particular concern remains the distribution of wealth. Bad times can make it even more unequal, with marginal businesses and households going over the edge. Assets then are there to be garnered at knock-down prices. The economy becomes more of a stock exchange. After the hiatus, employment will struggle to get back to the levels we are used to seeing. Once again the world is shown to be about adaption and flair; our edifices do not endure.

Modern Monetary Theory (MMT) offers a simple rearrangement to confront recession/depression. Money to bring the economy back to life – created by the government – is to be conceived of as a stimulus, not a debt. Like a citizen's income over a lean period. The principle is to match the money supply to the (desired) level of economic activity – carried out, importantly, by a public body. The rescue programme need not be ruinously inflationary on account of the extent of unused productive capacity. Simultaneously, one trusts that the virtuous circle of confidence in the economy is restored.

Many fine words have been uttered about the society we might have after this episode. These I take as signs of unease about where we were, and indications of more than a little reluctance to go back there. Indeed, some may now have chosen or welcomed other employment, or modified ways of life after insights gained in enforced isolation. Generally, coming out of the crisis, I expect priorities to be somewhat rearranged by experience of solidarity, goodwill and endurance, although memory tends to fade. Kindness is the first insurance for the community, and is always personally redemptive. Yet as stability and affluence creep back, pent-up demand will be released along with the desire to 'step out'. I don't blame humans. It is what we do. Just show other options that are able to channel these energies.

Life is complemented by cultivating an acceptance, healthy and philosophical, of death, and by making one's peace with the world. But in a culture driven by domination, death is regarded as tantamount to failure, just as shame and moral defect get pinned on illness. Much of our healing still has an uphill journey.

Time has also been filled with speculation about what work will look like. Videoconferencing has necessarily been more in action, saving on trips (junkets and jollys) that were not really necessary. Online orders were already transforming buying, to the point where many high streets could not hide the necrosis. If 'social distancing' is still in place, the trading model in sectors such as transport and hospitality will need overhauling – it is difficult to see how the present one will be viable. A visit to the dentist may have to look like a UFO abduction.

What must not be ignored, though, is that we need to be in enough of a natural environment for our abilities to function. In remote working a perception of things cannot be complete if one is not in their presence, and likewise professional interaction will not be as sophisticated and therefore less productive. This said, however, I cannot see the bricks-and-mortar, bums-on-seats university model, with its standard course structure, staying unchanged. Besides, this sector's operation at the current level was in question. Structurally the jobs are not there to justify many students' investment. In all likelihood one is looking at a bubble about to burst.

Climate change was already being broadcast as globally urgent. The focus, however, must be widened to include *environment* change. One shock may stimulate us to avoid another. If so, national economic recovery programmes will be weighted in favour of 'green' investment, even if projects are only green in very few (blazoned) respects. However, I doubt whether a higher order of caution here will be exercised on the other side of the virus. Reason produces only gradual change; it is revelation that projects us to another level. Already there is our bias towards the short-term, even when what amounts to denial is not present. An absurd example of this orientation is found in the story of the Easter Islanders, who cut down all their trees, thereby marooning themselves. (Doubtless too simple a telling, but wood for boats?) Moreover, a climate mayhem no-one has ever seen before has to join more familiar threats queuing up for attention. So provision for both prevention and preparation is likely to find itself short of cash when the fanfares have died down and the bravura evaporated. It would take a remarkable compliance, supported by an all-out defamation of alternative viewpoints, for it to be otherwise. Human willpower has a tendency to unwind also, reverting even to sloth, and the uppermost echelons of the power structure will almost certainly deem that strictures somehow do not apply to them; this much we know from history.

After what, at the time of writing, has been an effective 'lockdown' with majority assent, we will see whether the governors are tempted to hold on to some of the illiberalism. Certainly, the depth of our democracy has been shown to be lacking. (Not surprising, as I believe for human evolution to work most members of the group have to be 'followers'.) Unhappily this is a situation open to abuse and the toleration of incompetence. The policy of depriving everyone of their liberty instead of just insulating the statistically vulnerable groups was arguably too blunt an instrument. Public co-operation is indispensable for sustainable governance.

As for manner, ministers could be patronising or irritated. Not a lot of empathy or courtesy for the people, apart from cliché, was on show. I was a little surprised to see such elementary PR failings. Government failed to involve, openly, the popular mood in decisions as events unfolded. The word was that we would only cope with one simple message at a time. Discussion of an 'exit' strategy, for example, which could have helped bring the nation along, would have confused us, apparently. It is easy to be wise after the event but these things do betray administrative instincts. Listen out for the sound of the goalposts being moved.

The cornered politician is a curious spectacle. Mea culpa can be an effective tactic but is seldom deployed at the right time, leaving that individual a sitting target; an apology too late compounds the ordeal. Instead we are likely to see the tell-tale signs of lying – shallow breathing, tightness around the eyes, gazing into the distance, lack of sonority in the voice, a warping aura with acid colours and so on. It is a parade. It gets worse personally for these actors. Selfish actions weld us more firmly to this material plane, to continue to be beguiled by its ephemera. This is not to 'Know thyself'.

I accept that being economical with the truth goes, to a degree, with the job, but what destroys is the False Leader. These bods are rumbled eventually by events but their reigns are typified by divisiveness, lack of consultation, your submission as a condition for inclusion in society, unconstitutional punishments, policies flogged as dead horses, cruel sacrifice, spiel about the greater good, use of loaded terminology, trying it on with laughable smears and much more. This is the worst of the ego, and their finale can be them ranting with disbelief in palaces or bunkers. Recent times have seen quite a few of their smaller-scale ilk flushed out. Finally people's revulsion overcomes their fear and change is effected. Society requires major repairs, and one hopes that the archetypical sequence does not begin again too soon.

There is the end of Mussolini in Italy in 1945. The photographs show the bodies of himself and his mistress hung upside down in the Piazzale Loreto in Milan. Grisly, yes, but we humans like comeuppance to have some style. It is a formal announcement. Rough justice is undeniably cathartic, too.

A dispiriting observation is that, in the early stage of the dictatorship cycle, voters, in their longing, mistake the tyrant for a firm and decisive guide. By then they will already have given over too much of their responsibility. The demagogue exploits those who, psychologically speaking, have not taken on and integrated, within the family, the power of the father archetype.

The national effort is less when those who feel excluded from prosperity particularly, and from consideration generally, choose not to co-operate with government requests. One might expect to see this group also voting less. The immediate challenge is to bring these citizens back from this pique and hopelessness, with kept promises, not blarney.

Opposition politicians offered little of substance. True, the British Labour Party was busy being embarrassed by its association with the working-class but where was the rigorous questioning of the extraordinary deprivation of freedoms and its duration? The onus is always on government to make the case for a continuation of emergency measures, whilst parliament is to hold the executive to account. In the name of 'clarity', opposing parties also seemed reluctant to permit people to use common sense and the yardstick of the reasonable in applying guidelines to individual circumstances. This is at best paternalism. There is, ceteris paribus, an inverse relationship between the applicability of a rule and the complexity of the human environment. Their schtick was to launch, in the political bear garden, attack after attack over events past – however low in importance – when what was required was attention to the job in hand. Many MPs appear to forget that this brand of politicking really hacks off the public. The professional moaning was tiresome, the encouragement of a self-pity worse. The latter leads to violence; consuming's conditioning has already made us impatient. Media indulged the bickering, and a patent desire to verbally hurt. These spats may have been due, in part, to the unfortunate tendency of humans to turn on each other when the pressure becomes too great. Whatever, it is clear that we have some way to go before we can call ourselves a mature representative democracy. Sure signs that we have not got there are where debate is displaced by an ex-cathedra line and when other views activate the 'misinformation' alarm. It has been painful to look upon a BBC so cravenly 'on message'. That has been their betrayal.

Big Media has now been truly 'outed'. We got sick of the poison from what should have been the fourth estate. Its small set of crafted messages, intoned and repeated, made me think of a spell being cast. I learned two terms new to me recently: 'journaliars' and 'presstitutes'. The best thing one can say about its so-called journalists is that they asked the wrong questions over and over and preferred being right above everything else. They will still be dancing after the music has stopped.

As the story lumbered on the Labour opposition was even

more domineering in the measures it called for. No doubt political pundits would see this as a cynical attempt to out-compete the government in apparent resolve, and as such it can only have been for public consumption. And even a subliminal pitch to appear the benevolent father reassuring the bewildered children. However, illiberalism cannot pass muster as 'the common good'; the real carrier of life is the individual, according to Jung. The party clearly needs a radical adaptation of its principles to a world that has moved on. Actually there is still an important political space for it to occupy, preferably without deserting its traditional support. Providing voting has meaning.

Persistently instilling fear in people to obtain their consent to government policy will end up in a weak, regressed and unproductive country. Presenting deaths *with* Covid as deaths *from* Covid is the biggest scare tactic I have ever seen. In the coverage, anecdote got presented as statistical generality. They were not finished; the nigh-on useless wearing of masks represented subjugation and prodded people towards apologising for existing. I conclude that we did not love the truth enough, or did not recognise it as a calling.

The negation of discussion is silence, and that of the churches during these times will be remembered. Many people needed to be reminded of where the true strength lies, in a message that could be heard by non-believers too. There were two 'lockdowns'; the other one was of ideas.

How did we get to the point where a desire to examine the official narrative gets one accused of being a conspiracy nutjob? A demonisation today that may be a criminalisation tomorrow. But the Dalai Lama has observed that our enemies are our greatest teachers. Actually listening to them, according to Guy Wildwood, reduces significantly one's chances of being a chump. Still, in a lowered public discourse, shouting now appears to be accepted as argument. The questions remain, however. If there are no excess deaths where is the pandemic?

What pandemic is there if the tests are unreliable? Has the virus ever been isolated for that matter? Did computer models replace evidence from reality? Did the official scaremongering produce a nocebo effect (opposite of placebo) in health outcomes? Does vaccination always overreach itself and turn into a fetish? Does vaccination encourage the rise of variants? Can a plan of action become, metaphorically, trimming the jigsaw pieces to fit the puzzle? I believe that 'cancellation' is really about getting us to where we accept: 'War is peace. Freedom is slavery. Ignorance is strength' (George Orwell, *Nineteen Eighty-Four*).

Backed up by threats, it is not dissimilar to a protection racket. Talk is easier to police if words are taken literally, and the social milieu is not excepted. In fact verbal transgression, including a minor instance dragged up from your past, is enough to get you damned forever. I wonder when we will step out of this reign of terror. For now we have to inhabit a flatland swept by searchlights, so to speak.

Whether any vaccination programme is voluntary or mandatory will be a good indicator of political direction. Existing leadership has for some time sought to rub out vaccine dissent. Compulsory medication, or the blackmailing version of removing human rights if one does not comply, would contribute enormously to Statist power and end bodily autonomy. To the extent that those rights are removed when one chooses not to be inoculated, the vaccine is compulsory. On the other hand, offering inducements to accept a medical procedure is bribery, and shows the case for it has not been made. 'Jab', moreover, is a misuse of language, where 'experimental genetic implantation' is a more accurate term than 'vaccine'. A heap of harms has to be expected from a rushed programme. It is also unlikely that the opportunity to incorporate other things in and around the treatment would be passed up. Opportunism, employing pretext, is as much a threat as planned conspiracy, if not more so.

Doctors' judgement in the clinical setting is being usurped by guidelines from above. One size fitting all is lazy science, bad law and a blundering modality for a health service. This is authoritarianism in medicine, and like examples elsewhere it will run and run, until run out of town. Under it any old treatment can be enforced, backed up by a dreadful certitude and the fervour seen in a witch-hunt. Its like has a tendency to occur. A way to counteract this is for health provision to be based on the issuance of healthcare vouchers, redeemable either in an NHS or with practices, doctors and therapists independent within the scheme; finance follows footfall.

There remains a core of inalienable rights, so security cannot be founded on appeasement – we do not need to learn that lesson again. Also a right is paired with a responsibility. It is like taking a lavish limousine where you are both the (taciturn) chauffeur behind the wheel and the passenger lolling in the back.

Question. Is it a sensible use of resources to vaccinate a whole population for a disease that has a 99.8 per cent recovery rate, and where the average age of supposedly dying from it is in the eighties?

Evolutionary theory could be on our side, in that the virus should (but not necessarily) become milder with time; killing the host is not a strategy for enduring self-replication. Simultaneously, natural immunity will be mobilised. But a prescription that alters your genetic information is the beginning of transhumanism, by the way. Being made in the image, and after the likeness, of God (Genesis 1:26) constitutes a caution about what we allow to be done to our bodies.

The story is still unfolding, with its remarkable echoes of the mediaeval European dance mania. Will the dénouement be bungle or, despite the opposing force, coup? Our way of life is being rejigged, like it or not. Nationhood and tradition are assailed, citizen confidence chipped away at, and our instinct towards community used against us. The indigenous working-class is certainly a target; it is easy to list other ones. Subjective beliefs are claimed to be objective realities and causes become secular religions. Thought crime is now up there on the list of the most heinous. We now need a new edition of the dictionary of double-speak. Vague, fluffy terms like 'inclusivity', 'respect' and 'safety' all mean, in practice, conformity – of the type found in a police-state. A globalist authoritarianism rises like a new sun; the gulf between the people and the politicians is as big as I can remember. We humble folk tend to think in terms of two, three, possibly four, generations. The dynasts and despots work with extended projections, which gives them a key advantage in this class battle. Best to participate in the struggle by being the Light, capital 'l'. Try to refuse the blindfold at the firing squad.

It is deplorable to have the police brought in to enforce an unjust statute. Their behaviour at (some) Covid demonstrations does not appear to have changed. First, unprofessionalism amounts to a provocation of the protestors. Then, when there is the inevitable reaction, the black phalanx can wade in with its weapons. If brutality can ever be called pathetic, this is an example of it. The news orthodoxy is now able to label it a violent protest, thus delegitimising the people's genuine complaints. Deployment of the dedicated agent provocateur has not been necessary. Arrests and substantial fines follow. Job done all round.

The final destination for dissent and difference is the detention camp, that is if the thugs have not been turned on you first. The Tutsi in Rwanda never reached such places. Those who submit must realise that they can never be safe either. Under Stalin's reign it was wise to have a suitcase packed for when they came for you. Or maybe you would get a bullet while out on a pleasant country stroll. Robespierre was sent to Madame Guillotine by his own Revolution, and the members of a hit-squad may themselves be terminated following a mission so as to destroy evidence. If deniability is important there is the improbable accident or the theatre of the fake suicide.

In his 'Letter from Birmingham Jail', MLK affirmed that one has a moral responsibility to disobey unjust laws, a stance supported by the jury system where jurors can express displeasure with a particular law by acquitting a defendant technically guilty under it. Can we now be more expansive about who we are? As in the economic sphere 'Man shall not live by bread alone, but by every word that proceedeth out of the mouth of God' (Matthew 4:4). As always, put the word 'God' in inverted commas if that is truer to your understanding.

The great love affair is the one with that God.

It is worth saying that a submissive life is a wasted life. In the economy of the panopticon one is going to be a tolerated cipher or a pawn paid from petty cash.

If we get to the other side as a recognisable country there must be accountability for those who imposed Coronavirus measures that were disproportionate or that lacked logic, for those who ploughed on with failing rules and consequent rising rates of harm (direct and indirect), for those who ignored or suppressed other treatment protocols, and particularly for those who advanced other agendas under the guise of public benefit. After an occupation there is the question of what to do with the collaborators.

It could be that one of those periodic showdowns with the bad guys has come around in our lifetimes.

The times are dark but I can end on an entirely justified positive note. Each of us can choose to be a conscious part, open and constant, of the great circle of giving and receiving, which is the real economy. 'Give, and it shall be given unto you' (Luke 6:38) describes the perpetual exchange. The dynamic is glimpsed more in hard times, when deeper thanks take the place of routine and fleeting satisfactions. You have the warmest of welcomes to this other reset and the greater cosmic rhythm.

Select Bibliography and Further Reading

Peter Mark Adams, *The Power of the Healing Field: Energy Medicine, Psi Abilities, and Ancestral Healing*, Inner Traditions Audio, 2022 (Audible Audiobook).

Adyashanti, *Resurrecting Jesus: Embodying the Spirit of a Revolutionary Mystic*, Sounds True, 2014 (Audible Audiobook).

Dr Eben Alexander, *Proof of Heaven: A Neurosurgeon's Journey into the Afterlife*, Piatkus, 2012.

Dr Eben Alexander with Ptolemy Tompkins, *The Map of Heaven: A neurosurgeon explores the mysteries of the afterlife and the truth about what lies beyond*, Piatkus, 2014.

Anonymous, *Turtles All the Way Down: Vaccine Science and Myth*, The Turtles Team, 2024 (Audiobook, Audible).

Bruno Bettelheim, *The Uses of Enchantment: The Meaning and Importance of Fairy Tales*, CD, Tantor Media, Inc., 2017.

Martin Blank, *Overpowered: what science tells us about the dangers of cell phones and other Wifi-era devices*, Seven Stories Press, 2014.

Cynthia Bourgeault, *The Wisdom Jesus: Transforming Heart and Mind – a New Perspective on Christ and His Message*, Shambhala Publications, Inc., 2008.

Rutger Bregman, *Humankind: A Hopeful History*, CD, Hachette Audio, 2020.

James Bruges, *The Big Earth Book: Ideas and Solutions for a Planet in Crisis*, Alastair Sawday Publishing, 2007.

Ha-Joon Chang, *23 Things They Don't Tell You About Capitalism*, MP3-CD, Brilliance Audio, Audible, Inc., 2011.

Geoffrey Chaucer (translated into Modern English by Nevill Coghill), *The Canterbury Tales*, Cresset Press, 1992.

Noam Chomsky, *How The World Works*, interviewed by David Barsamian, edited by Arthur Naiman, Hamish Hamilton, 2012.

Barrie Condon, *Science for Heretics: Why so Much of Science is Wrong*, Sparsile Books Ltd, 2018.

John Davies, *A History of Wales*, Allen Lane The Penguin Press, 1993.

Charles Eisenstein, *Sacred Economics: Money, Gift and Society in the Age of Transition*, North Atlantic Books, 2011.

Daniel Estulin, *The Tavistock Institute: Social Engineering the Masses*, Trine Day LLC, 2015.

Stephen Ellcock, *All Good Things*, September Publishing, 2019.

Peter Fernando, *Finding Freedom in Illness: A Guide to Cultivating Deep Well-Being through Mindfulness and Self-Compassion*, MP3-CD, Brilliance Audio, Audible, Inc., 2016.

James Finley, *Meister Eckhart's Living Wisdom: Indestructible Joy and the Path of Letting Go*, Sounds True, 2014.

Ian Fitzgerald, *The Deep State: A History of Secret Agendas and Shadow Governments*, Arcturus Digital Limited, 2022 (Audible Audiobook).

Captain Jerry G. Flynn, *Hidden Dangers 5G: How governments, telecom and electric power utilities suppress the truth about the known hazards of electro-magnetic field (EMF) radiation*, JGF Publishing, 2019.

Paul Foot, *The Vote: How It was Won and How It was Undermined*, Bookmarks Publications, 2012.

Matthew Fox, *Radical Prayer: Love in Action*, Sounds True, CD, 2003.

Matthew Fox and Rupert Sheldrake, *The Physics of Angels: Exploring the Realm where Science and Spirit Meet*, HarperSanFrancisco, 1996.

Erich Fromm, *The Essential Fromm: Life Between Having and Being*, Tantor Audio, 2024 (Audible).

Gangaji, *The Diamond in Your Pocket*, Sounds True, CD, 2007.

David Graeber, *Bullshit Jobs*, CD, Simon and Schuster, Inc, 2018.

John Gray, *False Dawn: the Delusions of Global Capitalism*, Granta Books, 2002.

Geoffrey Grigson, *The Oxford Book of Satirical Verse*, Oxford University Press, 1980.

Stanislav Grof, *The Transpersonal Vision: The Healing Potential of Nonordinary States of Consciousness*, Sounds True, 1999 (Audible).

Heather Hamilton, *Returning to Eden: A Field Guide for the Spiritual Journey*, Quoir, 2023.

Gérald Hanotiaux, *Social Exclusion due to Electromagnetic Pollution: A Belgian Perspective*, Excerpts selected and translated from the French by Annelie Fitzgerald, ES-UK.

Yuval Noah Harari, *21 Lessons for the 21st Century*, CD, Random House Audio, 2018.

Andrew Harvey, *The Hope: A Guide to Sacred Activism*, Hay House, 2009.

Bud Harris, *Radical Hope and the Healing Power of Illness: A Jungian Guide to Exploring the Body, Mind, Spirit Connection to Healing*, Daphne Publications, 2017 (Audible).

Stephen R. C. Hicks, *Explaining Postmodernism: Skepticism and Socialism from Rousseau to Foucault*, Expanded Edition, Ockham's Razor Publishing, 2014.

Tom Holland, *Rubicon: The Triumph and Tragedy of the Roman Republic*, Hachette Audio, 2007.

The Derrick Jensen Reader: Writings on Environmental Revolution, edited by Lierre Keith, Seven Stories Press, 2012.

Stephanie Kelton, *The Deficit Myth: Modern Monetary Theory and the Birth of the People's Economy*, CD, Hachette Audio, 2020.

Alfie Kohn, *No Contest: The Case Against Competition*, Revised Edition, Houghton Mifflin Company, 1992.

Kenneth S. Leong, *The Zen Teachings of Jesus*, The Crossroad Publishing Company, 2001.

Peter A. Levine, *Healing Trauma: Restoring the Wisdom of the Body*, Sounds True, 1999 (Audiobook, Audible).

Paul Levy, *Dispelling Wetiko: Breaking The Curse of Evil*, North Atlantic Books, 2013.

Daniel E. Lieberman, *The Story of the Human Body: Evolution, Health and Disease*, Random House Audio, Random House LLC, 2013.

Thomas Mayer, *Overcoming Fear: Exercises for spiritual self-defense*, 2022.

Thomas Mayer, *Covid Vaccines from a Spiritual Perspective: Consequences for the Soul and Spirit and for Life after Death*, second edition, 2025.

Mark McDonald M. D., *United States of Fear: How America Fell Victim to a Mass Delusional Psychosis*, Bombardier Books, 2021.

David Michaels, *Doubt is Their Product: How Industry's Assault on Science Threatens Your Health*, Oxford University Press, 2008.

Marc Morano, *The Great Reset: Global Elites and the Permanent Lockdown*, Regnery Publishing, 2022 (Audible Audiobook).

Jeremy Naydler, *The Struggle for a Human Future: 5G, Augmented Reality and the Internet of Things*, Temple Lodge, 2020.

Alex Newman, *Indoctrinating Our Children to Death: Government Schools' War on Faith, Family, and Freedom – And How to Stop It*, Liberty Sentinel Press, 2024 (Audible Audiobook).

Michael Newton, *Journey of Souls: Case Studies of Life Between Lives*, MP3-CD, Tantor Media, Inc., 2011.

Michael Newton, *Destiny of Souls: New Case Studies of Life Between Lives*, CD, Tantor Media, Inc., 2011.

Paul Oliver, *World Faiths*, Teach Yourself, 2003.

Elaine Pagels, *The Gnostic Gospels*, CD, Random House Inc., 2006.

Jordan B. Peterson, *12 Rules for Life: An Antidote to Chaos*, CD, Penguin Books Ltd, 2018.

Jordan B. Peterson, *Beyond Order: 12 More Rules for Life*, Penguin Audio, 2021.

Joseph Plummer, *Tragedy and Hope 101: The Illusion of Justice, Freedom and Democracy*, Author's Republic, 2014 (Audible).

Aidan Rankin, *Many-Sided Wisdom: A New Politics of the Spirit*, O Books, 2010.

Sharon Hewitt Rawlette, *The Source and Significance of Coincidences: A Hard Look at the Astonishing Evidence*, 2019.

Michael Rectenwald, *The Great Reset and the Struggle for Liberty: Unraveling the Global Agenda*, New English Review Press, 2023.

Emrys Roberts, *Highlights from Welsh History: Opening Some Windows on Our Past*, Y Lolfa Cyf., 2017.

Richard Rohr, *Job and the Mystery of Suffering: Spiritual Reflections*, The Crossroad Publishing Company, 1996.

Richard Rohr, with Joseph Martos, *From Wild Man to Wise Man: Reflections on Male Spirituality*, St. Anthony Messenger Press, 2005.

Richard Rohr, *The Naked Now: Learning to see as the Mystics See*, Dreamscape Media, LLC, 2020 (Audible Audiobook).

Richard Rohr, *What Do We Do With the Bible?*, Audible Studios, 2020.

Richard Rohr, *Jesus' Alternative Plan: The Sermon on the Mount*, Franciscan Media, 2022 (Audible Audiobook).

Chris Rothman, *The Dictionary of Important Ideas and Thinkers*, Hutchinson, 2001.

Noah Rothman, *The Rise of the New Puritans: Fighting Back Against Progressives' War on Fun*, HarperCollins Publishers, 2022 (Audible Audiobook).

Shelley: Poems, Everyman's Library, 1993.

Ellis Silver, *Humans Are Not From Earth: a scientific evaluation of the evidence*, Second Edition, ideas4writers, 2017.

Ellis Silver, *SuperMars: Where We Really Came From And Where We'll Go When The World Ends*, ideas4writers, 2021.

Katie Singer, *An Electronic Silent Spring: Facing the Dangers and Creating Safe Limits*, Portal Books, 2014.

Martha Stout, *The Sociopath Next Door: The Ruthless Versus the Rest of Us*, Harmony Books, 2005.

Barry Strauss, *The Spartacus War*, Phoenix, 2010.

Frank Tallis, *The Act of Living: What the Great Psychologists Can Teach Us about Finding Fulfillment*, MP3 CD, Dreamscape Media, LLC, 2020.

Edward Vallance, *A Radical History of Britain: Visionaries, Rebels and Revolutionaries - The Men and Women Who Fought for Our Freedoms*, Little, Brown, 2009.

Arthur Waley, *The Way and its Power: The Tao Tê Ching and its place in Chinese Thought*, Mandala Books, 1977.

David Weir, *Decadence: A Very Short Introduction*, MP3-CD, Oxford University Press, 2018, Tantor Media, Inc., 2018.

Richard Wilkinson and Kate Pickett, *The Spirit Level: Why Equality is Better for Everyone*, Penguin Books, 2010.

Mark Wolynn, *It Didn't Start With You: How inherited family trauma shapes who we are and how to end the cycle*, Penguin Audio, 2022 (Audible Audiobook).

Paramahansa Yogananda, *The Yoga of the Bhagavad Gita: An Introduction to India's Universal Science of God-Realization*, Self-Realization Fellowship, 2007.

Paramahansa Yogananda, *The Yoga of Jesus: Understanding the Hidden Teachings of the Gospels*, Self-Realization Fellowship, 2007.

Theodore Zeldin, *The Hidden Pleasures of Life: A New Way of Remembering the Past and Imagining the Future*, CD, W.F. Howes Ltd, 2015.

Chambers English Dictionary, W and R Chambers Ltd, 1990.

Poems of Gratitude, edited by Emily Fragos, Everyman's Library, 2017.

The Bible. Authorized King James Version with Apocrypha, With an Introduction and Notes by Robert Carroll and Stephen Prickett, Oxford World's Classics, 2008.

The Bible Book, Dorling Kindersley, 2018.

The Economics Book, Dorling Kindersley, 2012.

The New Oxford Book of English Verse, chosen and edited by Helen Gardner, Oxford University Press, 1986.

The Oxford Dictionary of Quotations, Revised Fourth Edition, edited by Angela Partington, Oxford University Press, 1996.

The Penguin Dictionary of Epigrams, M.J. Cohen, Penguin Books, 2001.

The Philosophy Book, Dorling Kindersley, 2011.

The Politics Book, Dorling Kindersley, 2013.

The Author

Originally from Northamptonshire, England, Guy was educated at the Universities of Newcastle-upon-Tyne (Economics) and Lancaster (Systems in Management). Ill health necessitated another path, and he has worked both as a hospital porter and a theatre critic, amongst other things, as well as training at the College of Healing in Worcestershire. His most recent incarnation was as a home-educating dad living in Pembrokeshire, Wales, before producing this, his first and last book!

My Thanks

To Stuart Evans for his encouragement – to get on with writing this!

To Jo and Topaz for the support I needed, and for putting up with me during the book's creation when I was more preoccupied than present. (I was often speaking in writerly sentences, too.) More thanks to Jo for her artwork.

To Dewi Rhys-Jones for his guidance and for taking the time.

To Peter Lloyd for turning into a consultant in readership response.

To Christine Foley for typing and presenting the manuscript.

To Janice Casey at Little Red Fox Design (07582 438 567) for giving this, as it were, fine garments for the journey – in place of the T-shirt, jeans and trainers it turned up in.

To the nice people at Y Lolfa. To Lefi Gruffudd for going for the project, and to my editor Eirian Jones for presenting this voice, my voice. To designer Alan Thomas also. It was a pleasure working with you. Diolch yn fawr, unwaith eto.

And to the giants on whose shoulders I have been able to stand.